THIS
OR
THAT?
3

or

or

EVEN MORE WACKY CHOICES
TO REVEAL THE
HIDDEN
YOU

JR MORTIMER & NANCY CASTALDO

NATIONAL
GEOGRAPHIC
KiDS

WASHINGTON, D.C.

The National Geographic Society is one of the world's largest non-profit scientific and educational organizations. Founded in 1888 to "increase and diffuse geographic knowledge," the Society's mission is to inspire people to care about the planet. It reaches more than 400 million people worldwide each month through its official journal, *National Geographic*, and other magazines; National Geographic Channel; television documentaries; music; radio; films; books; DVDs; maps; exhibitions; live events; school publishing programs; interactive media; and merchandise. National Geographic has funded more than 10,000 scientific research, conservation, and exploration projects and supports an education program promoting geographic literacy.

For more information, please visit nationalgeographic.com, call 1-800-NGS LINE (647-5463), or write to the following address:
National Geographic Society
1145 17th Street N.W.
Washington, D.C. 20036-4688 U.S.A.

Visit us online at nationalgeographic.com/books

For librarians and teachers: ngchildrensbooks.org

More for kids from National Geographic: kids.nationalgeographic.com

For information about special discounts for bulk purchases, please contact National Geographic Books Special Sales: ngspecsales@ngs.org

For rights or permissions inquiries, please contact National Geographic Books Subsidiary Rights: ngbookrights@ngs.org

Library of Congress Cataloging-in-Publication Data

Mortimer, J. R.
  This or that? 3 : even more wacky choices to reveal the hidden you/
by J R Mortimer and Nancy Castaldo.
    pages cm
  ISBN 978-1-4263-1881-8 (pbk. : alk. paper) -- ISBN 978-1-4263-1882-5 (reinforced library binding : alk. paper)
  1. Life skills--Juvenile humor. I. Castaldo, Nancy F. (Nancy Fusco), 1962- II. Title.
  PN6231.L49M68 2015
  305.234--dc23
  2014036087

Printed in the United States of America
15/QGT-CML/1

TABLE OF CONTENTS

Introduction 6

Pack Your Bags 8

Sensational Superpowers! 28

Unsolved Mysteries 46

Gross Guts 64

Party Time! 82

Win or Lose 100

Silly Stats 118

Go-Go Gadgets 136

Trick or Treat? 154

Credits 174

GET PICKY!

CHOOSE **THIS:**
Watch a TV show after school.

CHOOSE **THAT:**
Tackle your home-work right away.

CHOOSE **THIS:**
Learn a musical instrument.

CHOOSE **THAT:**
Practice a new sport.

CHOOSE **THIS:**
Hang out with friends on the weekend.

CHOOSE **THAT:**
Do chores for some extra cash.

DECISIONS! DECISIONS!

Every minute of every day we make choices about how we spend our time, what we like, and how we interact with one another. Most are minor, but when you add them all up, your decisions reveal what makes you *you!* THIS or THAT? WHICH WILL IT BE?

WELCOME TO THE BOOK OF CHOICES. Want to find out what superpowers would suit you? Or maybe you'd like to know what countries you'd enjoy on a trip around the world? Each chapter offers you a series of options—some silly, some serious, some down-right spectacular, and some a little gross. Consider your choices with your friends—or even Mom or Dad—before you make up your mind. Then, read on to see where your decision leads.

DECISION DISSECTION!

KEEP COUNT
OF EACH TIME YOU CHOOSE

THIS!
or THAT!

AT THE END OF EACH CHAPTER, you'll get some professional help from **Dr. Matt Bellace**. He's a **stand-up comic**, a **motivational speaker**, and a **psychologist**. Dr. Bellace will analyze your choices and determine what your decisions say about you. Through exploration and analysis of the inner workings of your mind, he'll peel you back layer by layer and **you won't even realize it!** Don't worry about making a wrong choice—there are none. If you've ever been called picky, get ready for loads of fun!

IN THIS OR THAT? 3, IT'S A GOOD THING!

CHAPTER **1**

PACK YOUR BAGS

There are 195 countries in the world—why are you just sitting there? Go out and explore! From Albania to Zimbabwe, there are plenty of interesting—and weird—places you need to see! Shoo, now. Shoo!

THIS:

Play **hide-and-seek** with **mummies.**

or

THAT:

Have a sleepover **in** a **vampire's** castle.

MUSE BEFORE YOU CHOOSE Ancient curses. Getting lost in a pyramid. Blood loss. Annoying bats.

If you CHOSE ⬇THIS:

The mummies are hiding and you're doing the seeking if you pay a visit to the TIMBAC CAVES in the northern Philippines, the home of the famous FIRE MUMMIES. The mummified human remains were stashed here in man-made caves about 800 years ago by the Ibaloi tribe, and many of the mummies remain to this day. But good luck trying to find these DRIED-OUT CORPSES—the exact locations of most of the caves are kept unpublicized to prevent vandalism. They have been designated as one of the 100 most endangered sites in the world.

If you CHOSE ⬇THAT:

You and your friends are likely to never forget a night at BRAN CASTLE, the alleged home of Bram Stoker's bloodsucking character, DRACULA. Located in central Romania, the 13th-century fortress was supposedly the inspiration for the vampire's castle, even though BRAM STOKER NEVER ACTUALLY VISITED IT. The castle is currently a museum, and as of 2014, Bran Castle was up for sale for $80 million!

Bran Castle

Choice Nugget

Rumor has it that Mary Shelley found inspiration for her novel *Frankenstein* at the ruins of the real Frankenstein Castle near Frankfurt, Germany. If you're there in October, you'll see all kinds of ghouls and monsters lurking about at the Halloween festival.

CHOOSE THIS:

Visit an underwater museum.

Cancún underwater museum

or

CHOOSE THAT:

Tour a museum in the sky.

MUSE BEFORE YOU CHOOSE

Holding your breath. Fish friends. Fear of heights. Lightning strikes.

If you CHOSE THIS:

You'll need to strap on a scuba tank when you visit **MUSA**, a museum under the waters surrounding Cancún, Mexico. Created by a collaboration of several artists, over 500 actual-size human figures serve as **ARTIFICIAL REEFS**, attracting many kinds of coral, plants, and fish. The goal of the underwater museum is to raise awareness about the impact of pollution on natural coral reefs, which have diminished significantly in the past few decades. The **SCULPTURES** change over time as the coral spreads across their bodies and sea stars take up residence. You can swim through the museum every year and it will be different!

If you CHOSE THAT:

Empire State Building

You'll take an elevator all the way to the 80th floor to tour the museum at the **EMPIRE STATE BUILDING** in New York City. At 103 stories, the skyscraper stood as the world's tallest building for more than 40 years once it was completed in 1931. At the **MUSEUM'S** exhibit, you'll learn all about how the building was constructed from limestone trucked in from Indiana and how it was all finished in less than 15 months. Be sure to check out the **OBSERVATION DECKS** on the 86th and 102nd floors—it's a view that will truly take your breath away!

CHOOSE
THIS:
Crawl around **inside** an **elephant** and **come** out **alive.**

Lucy the Elephant

or

CHOOSE
THAT:
Keep your **distance** and **watch** an **elephant** with **binoculars.**

MUSE BEFORE YOU CHOOSE

Running out of oxygen. Claustrophobia. Elephants probably look better on the outside.

If you CHOSE ⬇ THIS:

You won't have to worry about getting stuck inside an **ELEPHANT** when you visit **LUCY** in Margate, New Jersey, U.S.A. She's a six-story building constructed out of wood and tin to look like an Asian elephant. Built in 1881 by James V. Lafferty, Jr., the **STRUCTURE** was one of three elephant-shaped buildings Lafferty built, but only Lucy has withstood the test of time. Over the years, Lucy has served as a restaurant, a cottage, and a tavern and has even survived getting struck by **LIGHTNING!**

If you CHOSE ⬇ THAT:

African elephants

Feel free to use your binoculars, but you may not need them when you visit Chobe National Park in **BOTSWANA.** The park is home to a large herd of African elephants—some 70,000 roam the land! The elephants here are called Kalahari, which is the largest of all known elephant **SUBSPECIES.** Be on the lookout as your safari group drives across the **PLAINS** because you never know when an elephant will stick out its trunk and say *hellurrrrrrr!*

CHOOSE THIS:

Train to **dig** up dinosaur **bones.**

or

CHOOSE THAT:

Train to **fly** among the **stars.**

MUSE BEFORE YOU CHOOSE

Dirty fingernails. Find a *T. rex*! Explore new worlds. Nausea.

If you CHOSE ⬇THIS:

You don't have to be a professional **PALEONTOLOGIST** to dig up dinosaur bones. The gullies and buttes in North Dakota and the badlands of South Dakota are rich with **FOSSILS** dating back millions of years to when this part of the United States was under water. Be sure to go on a **"PALEO-ADVENTURE,"** an expedition where knowledgeable guides show you how to spot fossils in the earth and how to remove them safely. Digging up fossils takes a lot of time and patience, so be prepared to put in some hours in the **HOT** sun. But who knows, you may find an unknown species and all that effort will be well worth it!

mammoth skull in the Black Hills, South Dakota, U.S.A.

If you CHOSE THAT: ⬇

If working in **ZERO GRAVITY** interests you, head over to Houston, Texas, U.S.A., where you'll find NASA's **NEUTRAL BUOYANCY LAB.** Astronauts are trained in a vast pool that holds 6.2 million gallons (about 23.5 million L) of water. **NASA** considers working underwater a great way to prepare future **ASTRONAUTS** for the **WEIGHTLESSNESS** of space. In the water, the astronauts can be weighted properly so they neither sink to the bottom nor rise to the top—even if they *do* weigh 350 pounds (159 kg) in their suits!

NASA Neutral Buoyancy Lab

THIS:

Go where **north** meets **south.**

or

Marco Zero, Macapá, Brazil

CHOOSE

THAT:

Go where **east** meets **west.**

EAST

WEST

MUSE BEFORE YOU CHOOSE Which cardinal direction suits your fancy?

18

If you CHOSE ⬇THIS:

Just like your compass does everywhere else, it will still point north when you're in **MACAPÁ**, a city in Brazil that is split in two by the **EQUATOR**. Few roads go in or out of Macapá, making it a little hard to get to, but once you're there you should check out the Monumento do Marco Zero. It's a large sundial that stands directly on the imaginary line that divides the Northern and Southern **HEMISPHERES** of the globe. People gather at the monument twice a year to watch the **EQUINOX**— the moment when the plane of the Earth's Equator passes the center of the sun. Be sure to bring your sunglasses!

If you CHOSE ⬇THAT:

Your left foot could be in the Western Hemisphere and your right foot could be in the Eastern Hemisphere when you're in **GREENWICH, ENGLAND**. It's the location of the prime meridian, the imaginary line used to indicate **ZERO DEGREES** longitude. Back in 1884, an international conference was held in Washington, D.C., to establish a "vertical equator" that would be helpful in ship navigation, and they decided on Greenwich, England. Since then, Greenwich has been the basis for the world's **STANDARD TIME ZONES**. As you move 15 degrees longitude east, the time is one hour later. Keep that in mind on your travels!

Greenwich, England

CHOOSE THIS:

Stand in the **shoes** of a **famous painter.**

or

CHOOSE THAT:

Follow the **path** of a famous **photographer.**

MUSE BEFORE YOU CHOOSE   Staring at flowers for *long* periods of time. Trekking through the wilderness.

If you CHOSE ⬇THIS:

Take a stroll outside the house of painter **CLAUDE MONET** in Giverny, France, and you're likely to be inspired by the colorful **GARDENS** and **PONDS**. Monet and his family lived in the house for 43 years—from 1883 to 1926—and over that period they continued building rooms as the artist became more successful, even converting a barn into his studio. It was here on these grounds where the famous Impressionist painter created many beautiful **MASTERPIECES** that are now some of the most valuable artworks in history. In June 2014 a Monet painting of **WATER LILIES** sold for over $52 million! Who knows? Make a name for yourself as an artist and maybe one of your masterpieces will be worth that much one day!

"Monet's Garden" exhibition at the New York Botanical Gardens

If you CHOSE THAT: ⬇

You'll need more than just a camera if you follow in the footsteps of photographer **ANSEL ADAMS**—you'll need hiking boots too! That's because you'll be tramping through the rugged terrain of **YOSEMITE NATIONAL PARK** in California, U.S.A., an area that Adams photographed beginning in the 1920s. Stretching across the western slopes of the **SIERRA NEVADA MOUNTAINS**, the park has some of the world's most popular rock-climbing destinations. If you decide to brave the steep slopes, be sure your camera is strapped on good and tight. You wouldn't want to **LOSE IT** down a cliff!

Grand Teton National Park, photographed by Ansel Adams, 1942

CHOOSE THIS:

Visit a country that has no cities.

or

CHOOSE THAT:

Visit a country that is within a city.

Republic of Nauru

MUSE BEFORE YOU CHOOSE

Peace and quiet. No pollution. No picturesque farmlands. No fresh air.

Vatican City

flag of Nauru

If you CHOSE THIS:

You won't find a bustling **METROPOLIS** on the tiny island nation of **NAURU**, in the South Pacific. It is one of the world's smallest republics—so small in fact that its flag is literally a map showing people where to find it next to the **EQUATOR**. With only about 10,000 inhabitants, Nauru has no need for skyscrapers. Instead, Nauru's claim to fame is that the island was once entirely covered in **BIRD POOP**, which made the soil rich in phosphates that could be harvested and sold to other countries. But don't worry about the bird poop spoiling your trip—it ran out years ago!

If you CHOSE THAT:

VATICAN CITY has only about 840 citizens, but that doesn't mean you won't have to deal with crowded streets while you're there. Over five million visitors make their way to this tiny, walled-off country located within the city of Rome, Italy—often for its stunning art alone. The country is the domain of the **CATHOLIC CHURCH** and its leader, the **POPE**, and for many centuries, the church has funded some of history's most treasured artworks. Be sure to check out Michelangelo's ceiling at the Sistine Chapel—it took him four years to complete it!

Think Twice! Vatican City has one thing in common with the Republic of Nauru: bird poop! In Vatican City, pigeon poop can actually cause damage to the country's centuries-old architecture.

CHOOSE THIS:

Surf some gnarly **waves.**

or

CHOOSE THAT:

Play miniature golf in the **dark.**

MUSE
BEFORE YOU
CHOOSE

Break a record. Break a leg. Miss the ball. Hit somebody with the club.

If you CHOSE ⬇THIS:

You might want to have your brain checked if you hop on a **SURFBOARD** at Shipstern Bluff in Tasmania. Known for being one of the wildest and most **DANGEROUS** surf spots in the world, this area off the coast of Australia attracts only the most adventurous thrill seekers. It's got everything you should be afraid of! The waves are **HUGE** and slam into granite **BOULDERS** and coral reefs with tremendous force ... and huge great white sharks lurk just beneath the waves ... and the nearest hospital is four hours away! If that's not a recipe for disaster, then what is?

If you CHOSE THAT:⬇

As if getting a hole in one wasn't hard enough, try getting one in the **DARK!** That's what you can expect on your visit to **WILD ABYSS MINI-GOLF** in Wisconsin Dells, Wisconsin, U.S.A. You'll play through an underwater-themed golf course that is lit up with **BLACK LIGHTS**, which make neon-painted sea creatures explode with color. But that's not the only distraction you'll have to overcome to win the game. Try your best to focus on aiming the ball when you've got real sea life looking over your shoulder. The golf course has **AQUARIUMS** filled with real stingrays, eels, barracudas—and even sharks!

25

ANALYZE
THIS!

If you mostly picked **CHOOSE THIS,** you're probably a lone wolf type who isn't afraid to go it alone. You're an independent thinker, and you don't feel like you need to rely on others to make decisions. However, one possible downside to this type of personality is that you might keep people at arm's length. You thrive on solitary activities, like painting and surfing, which is great! Just remember, it's not bad to lean on your friends sometimes and ask for help.

ANALYZE
THAT!

If you mostly picked **CHOOSE THAT,** you're the life of the party! You thrive in social situations and get some exhilaration from them. The idea of taking risks, like visiting spooky or faraway places, is nothing as long as you're with someone. You like to feel connected with the world around you. It's likely that you grew up in a large family with a couple of pets, or ten. The more the merrier you say. The only downside to all of this socializing is there's little room to think. Remember, take time for yourself occasionally and just sit in silence, if you can find some.

CHAPTER 2

SENSATIONAL SUPER-POWERS!

Imagine you have the amazing superpowers of the Justice League or the X-Men. Each page in this chapter offers you a choice between two terrific superpowers. Turn the page to find out which superpowers suit you best!

CHOOSE THIS:

Your **powerful jaw** can **chomp** through **anything.**

or

CHOOSE THAT:

You **can drink** through your **skin.**

MUSE BEFORE YOU CHOOSE

No more nutcrackers needed. No more water bottles to carry.

If you CHOSE ⬇THIS:

You might not want to eat steel, but having a jaw **POWERFUL** enough to bite through something that hard works out very well for the giant panda. The panda's round head holds a set of **POWERFUL JAW** muscles that make it easy to munch down on thick bamboo stalks—stalks that are so tough that some can withstand compression even **BETTER THAN CONCRETE!** A giant panda spends about 12 hours a day eating bamboo. Chomp.

giant panda

If you CHOSE THAT:⬇

You would never have to worry about becoming dehydrated with a **GREEN FROG'S SUPERSKIN**, as long as you lived in a moist, wetland spot. A frog's skin absorbs **MOISTURE**, and these amphibians also rely on it for getting oxygen from the water they live in. Of course, they don't have too much choice about the water their skin absorbs. So frog-get swimming in chlorine pools!

green frog

THIS:

You can **jump 50** times **higher** than **your** own **body** length.

or

THAT:

You can **fly 385** body lengths **per** second.

MUSE BEFORE YOU CHOOSE Weird pole vault champion. Lots of exercise.

If you CHOSE ⬇THIS:

Imagine being able to jump 50 times your body length. **JUMPING SPIDERS** take this amazing ability in stride. Who needs a web when you can land on unsuspecting prey? These spiders are found all over the planet, even on **MOUNT EVEREST.** There are over 43,000 species. That's not so good for the millions of people who have **ARACHNOPHOBIA,** the fear of spiders. The good news is that jumping spiders don't see us as food, and some of them can actually be pretty cute!

▲ jumping spider

If you CHOSE THAT:⬇

Think of how fast you could travel if you could fly 385 body lengths per second. That's faster than a fighter jet, which can fly only 150 body lengths per second. **HUMMINGBIRDS** dart so fast you can barely see them when they're flying! They are the only animals capable of **SUSTAINED HOVERING.** They can also fly in any direction—up, down, backward, and upside down! Think of the places you could visit with that ability!

Think Twice!

Most ruby-throated hummingbirds fly from North America to Central America for the winter. Those tiny birds fly over 20 miles (32 km) a day!

◀ broad-billed hummingbird

33

CHOOSE THIS:

You're super fast, but you're in constant danger of being squashed.

or

CHOOSE THAT:

MUSE
BEFORE YOU
CHOOSE

Look out above!
Strange odors.

You have a super sense of smell, but your bite causes a slow death.

If you CHOSE THIS:

Even **MERCURY**, the god from **ROMAN MYTHOLOGY**, might not be as fast as a cockroach. If you could move as fast as a **COCKROACH**, you could run a 100-yard (91-m) dash in one second. With this superpower you could almost be in two places at once! Unfortunately, cockroaches don't have a fan club like **THE FLASH** does. They tend to be the main targets of the pest-removal industry!

If you CHOSE THAT:

You might be able to escape the jaws of the **KOMODO DRAGON**, but its bite can still kill you. New research by Dr. Bryan Fry of the University of Queensland, in Australia, has confirmed that Komodo dragons do in fact have **VENOM**—venom that causes a slow death. It decreases the victim's blood pressure, prevents blood clotting, and sends the victim into shock, making it too weak to fight back. The Komodo dragon tracks its dying prey from up to 2.5 miles (4 km) away using its super sense of **SMELL**. Talk about a leisure lunch. Yikes!

Komodo dragon

CHOOSE THIS:

You can **live** forever.

or

CHOOSE THAT:

You can **come back** from the **dead**.

MUSE BEFORE YOU CHOOSE

Outlive your friends. Time traveler.

If you CHOSE
↓THIS:

Imagine having lived so long that the great pyramids of Egypt were built during your toddler years. The Methuselah Tree, a **BRISTLECONE PINE** living in the White Mountains of California, U.S.A., has been growing for nearly **5,000 YEARS**! That's not exactly forever, but who knows how long it will be able to live. It is still producing seeds that sprout!

ancient bristlecone pine at Methuselah Grove, White Mountains, California, U.S.A.

If you CHOSE THAT: ↓

When scientists found an **ANCIENT DATE** seed in an archaeology site in Israel, radiocarbon dating of the seed's DNA determined that it was about **2,000 YEARS OLD**. The variety of date tree it dropped from has since become extinct. Scientists didn't let that deter them from trying to sprout the seed. They were successful and now have plans to **CROSSBREED** the plant with its closest living relative. You should be excited because the dates from this tree were famed for being super tasty.

DATES ...

Choice Nugget

An 80,000-year-old colony of quaking aspen trees is living in Fishlake National Forest, Utah, U.S.A. The trees—roughly 40,000 of them—aren't that old themselves, but their root system, known as Pando, or the Trembling Giant, is perhaps the oldest and largest organism on the planet.

CHOOSE

THIS:

You can have **fearsome armored** skin.

or

CHOOSE

THAT:

Your **skin** can **glow** in the **dark**.

jellyfish

MUSE
BEFORE YOU
CHOOSE

Ultimate fighter. Party animal.

If you CHOSE ⬇THIS:

Medieval knights wore **HEAVY ARMOR** on their bodies to protect them in battle. Imagine how agile and fearsome you could be with light armor. Delicate-looking **SEAHORSES** have squishable armor on their tails to protect them from being **CRUSHED** by predators. Researchers at the University of California, San Diego, in the United States, would like to build a robotic arm that mimics the seahorse's strong, flexible tail.

seahorse

If you CHOSE ⬇THAT:

Think of how cool you would be at parties with a **GREEN GLOW**, but on the downside, this super-power doesn't come with an off switch! Scientists in Hawaii, U.S.A., and Turkey have inserted naturally glowing jellyfish protein into rabbit embryos to create the first glowing **GENETICALLY MODIFIED BUNNIES**. The two bunnies look normal in daylight but glow bright green under black light. The green glow has no value other than to show the researchers if their experiment was a success and which rabbits have acquired the gene. In the future they may introduce **GENES** that could produce proteins in the bunny's milk that could be used as medicines.

Choice Nugget

In 2007, scientists in South Korea created a set of glowing cats by altering their DNA.

rabbit

39

CHOOSE THIS:

You can climb rock walls like Spider-Man.

or

CHOOSE THAT:

You can see in every direction without moving your head.

MUSE BEFORE YOU CHOOSE

Window washer? Ultimate spy.

If you CHOSE ⬇THIS:

Alpine ibex

CLIMBING GOATS have become an Internet sensation. It seems they'll climb anything, including smooth-looking 160-foot (49-m) dam **WALLS.** What seems impossible actually isn't for these super climbers. Wild goats called **ALPINE IBEXES** have adapted to the usual rocky mountain slopes they live on. The goats' hooves are split (cloven) to help them maintain balance and have a soft inner padding to aid with traction, and the animals have a low center of **GRAVITY.**

If you CHOSE THAT:⬇

No, you don't have another pair of eyes on the back of your head, but you can see who's coming and going with a **CHAMELEON'S** superpower 360-degree vision. Their eyes, on either side of their head, move independently allowing them to point in different directions. Their specially mounted eyes give them the ability to see **PREY** from all angles and also provide them with the binocular front vision needed to aim and **STRIKE!**

◀ Parson's chameleon

CHOOSE THIS:

You are the ultimate strongman.

dung beetle

MUSE BEFORE YOU CHOOSE

It's a dirty job, but someone has to do it. Catch me if you can.

or

CHOOSE THAT:

You can be a super shape-shifter.

If you CHOSE THIS:

Think of what you could do with superhuman strength, like the Incredible Hulk's. A **DUNG BEETLE,** the **STRONGEST** animal on Earth compared to its body weight, can pull something over 1,000 times its weight. That's like an average adult human pulling six full double-decker buses. And how do dung beetles use their **SUPREME STRENGTH?** Why, to fight rivals, of course! They also use it to roll up balls of animal dung, or **POOP,** which female dung beetles use as an egg-laying site or as food.

If you CHOSE THAT:

MIMICRY would enable you to copy anyone, so you could swim as fast as an Olympic athlete or write the next Harry Potter novel. Pretty cool, right? Animals do this all the time, but not to win any medals. They **DO IT TO SURVIVE!** Take the pebble plant that mimics stones so that it doesn't get eaten. Or the praying mantis that resembles flowers so that it can **ATTRACT PREY.** Creatures that use mimicry might use smell, sound, or behavior to copy a creature or object.

praying mantis

ANALYZE THIS!

If you mostly picked **CHOOSE THIS,** you're a person who values individual strength and personal accomplishments. If I were to look through your room right now, I suspect I'd find records of your athletic performances, including batting averages from Little League, or video game high scores. You may be the only one who cares about that stuff, but it's proof that you're trying to discover the limits of your abilities. You know that you're going to live up to your potential in life, and you're trying everything to make sure the sky is the limit.

ANALYZE THAT!

If you mostly picked **CHOOSE THAT,** you're a deep thinker who values things that others dismiss. Tough guys and girls don't impress you, because attention to detail is your secret strength. In fact, you're probably working hard every day building skills that other people your age have little interest in. You know that this investment will pay off in time. The day will come when the world will appreciate your skills. That's the day that people start calling you another name: "Boss"!

CHAPTER 3

UNSOLVED MYSTERIES

We live in a world where strange things have been known to happen. From UFO sightings to lost treasures, there are many questions we may never know the answers to. This chapter is all about the mysteries that keep us puzzled.

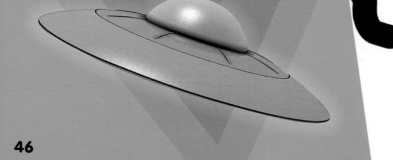

CHOOSE THIS:

Look out an airplane window at strange animals.

Nasca lines hummingbird

or

CHOOSE THAT:

Go scuba diving and follow a road to nowhere.

MUSE BEFORE YOU CHOOSE

Cool zoo in the sky. Fear of heights. See exotic fish. Sharks!

If you CHOSE THIS:

Hop in an airplane if you want to see the ancient **NASCA LINES** found in southern Peru, which were created between 500 B.C. and A.D. 500. The Nasca lines consist of hundreds of figures of varying complexity, including **HUMMINGBIRDS**, **SPIDERS**, **MONKEYS**, and **LIZARDS**. What's most impressive is the size of the drawings— the largest figures are over 660 feet (200 m) across! Archaeologists believe the lines were formed by removing the dark stones on the **DESERT** surface, which exposed the lighter sand beneath. However, no one is entirely certain why the Nasca people created such large artwork. Some scholars believe the lines have religious significance, while some fringe theorists believe they were an airport for **ALIENS**!

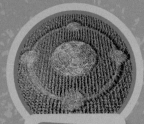

Choice Nugget

A crop circle is a pattern created by the flattening of a crop such as wheat or barley. These massive designs show up mysteriously in farmers' fields, leading some to believe they are messages from UFOs!

If you CHOSE THAT:

Put on a wet suit and explore the **BIMINI ROAD**, a mysterious underwater rock formation in the Bahamas. The straight line of rocks is nearly half a mile (0.8 km) in length and is composed of mostly rectangular blocks. The perfection of the blocks almost looks **HUMAN-MADE**, which has led some theorists to believe Bimini Road is the remains of an **ANCIENT CIVILIZATION**, maybe even Atlantis! If you ask geologists or archaeologists, they are likely to tell you the formation is a natural feature composed of beach rock with joints that have broken into rectangular blocks.

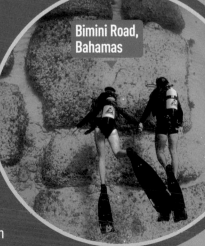

Bimini Road, Bahamas

CHOOSE **THIS:**

Roll around **in** a money **pit** that has **no money** in it.

or

CHOOSE **THAT:**

Go on an **egg hunt** that doesn't involve **edible** eggs.

Getting out may be a challenge. Make a discovery.
No snacking. Might find a prize egg.

If you CHOSE ⬇THIS:

You wouldn't want to do much rolling around in the "**MONEY PIT**" found on Oak Island in Nova Scotia, Canada. In 1795, a boy discovered a depression in the soil that was covered with flat stones. Thinking he had come across **BURIED TREASURE**, he and his friends dug up the stones and found layers of logs every ten feet (3 m), mixed with charcoal and coconut fibers, which was particularly strange since coconut is not a plant you'd find in Canada. Exhausted, the boys gave up after digging 30 feet (9 m) down. But ever since that mysterious discovery more than **200 YEARS** ago, treasure hunters have spent small fortunes trying to reach the bottom of the pit.

If you CHOSE THAT: ⬇

You'll be rewarded handsomely if you find one of the seven missing **FABERGÉ IMPERIAL EASTER EGGS** that disappeared nearly 100 years ago. Every Easter, a famous jeweler named Peter Carl Fabergé would present the Russian tsar with a very special gift: an egg crafted from **GOLD** and precious stones. But in 1917, Russia endured a political revolution and some of the eggs went missing. One of these eggs resurfaced in 2013 when an American man unwittingly bought it for $14,000, intending to sell it for scrap. When he couldn't find a buyer, he began searching on the Internet to learn more details. He was surprised to find out his egg was last seen in 1902 and was estimated to be worth **TENS OF MILLIONS** of dollars! Talk about an egg-cellent discovery!

Fabergé Imperial Easter egg

THIS:

Have a bloodsucking pet.

or

THAT:

Be friends with a birdlike giant.

Sharp fangs. Going for walks is awkward.
Free flights. Bullies won't mess with you.

If you CHOSE ⬇THIS:

Good luck trying to catch the sneaky **CHUPACABRA**, a legendary monster of the Americas that is said to attack and **DRINK** the **BLOOD** of livestock. The chupacabra is supposedly the size of a small bear, standing four feet (1.3 m) high, with spines from its neck to its tail. It is a reptile-like creature with leathery gray or greenish skin that hops like a kangaroo. Skeptics claim that the chupacabra is merely a **LEGEND** formed by sightings of wild dogs or other animals that suffer from mange, a skin disease caused by **PARASITIC MITES.** Either way—dog or monster—don't think for a second you can keep it as a pet!

If you CHOSE ⬇THAT:

You may want to reconsider getting friendly with the **MOTHMAN** of Point Pleasant, West Virginia, U.S.A., if you ever encounter him. First spotted in the 1960s, the **BIRDLIKE CREATURE** is almost 7 feet (2 m) tall and has glowing red eyes. It is said he has a wingspan of over 15 feet (4.5 m)! The local people believe the Mothman is associated with tragedy, as sightings tend to occur before major **CATASTRO-PHES,** like bridge collapses. While some say he is a mutant creature spawned from **TOXIC CHEMICALS,** skeptics usually dismiss the monster as a hoax or mass illusion. Regardless of whether the Mothman is real or not, the legend brings many tourists to the small town, so the locals don't mind him one bit!

Choice Nugget

Loogaroos are legendary creatures in the West Indies that suck the blood of innocent victims to obtain magical powers from the devil. They are believed to be able to shape-shift into other monsters. Are they real?

CHOOSE THIS: →

Stay up **late** and watch **strange** lights appear in the **desert.**

or

CHOOSE THAT: →

Spend an afternoon **with** a **cranky** **ghost** in a **cemetery.**

MUSE BEFORE YOU CHOOSE

Observe a rare occurrence. Alien abduction.
Get a thrilling spook! Paranormal attacks.

If you CHOSE ⬇THIS:

Forget having a bedtime if you want to see the MARFA LIGHTS, a strange phenomenon that occurs after dark in southwestern TEXAS, U.S.A. Since the 19th century, people have reported seeing brightly glowing spheres floating above the ground in the distance or high in the air. Sometimes yellow or white in color, the balls are said to appear in groups or pairs, and will ZOOM across the desert at astonishing speeds. Some people believe the Marfa lights are evidence for the existence of UFOs, but skeptics say that one explanation is that they are merely reflections of car headlights from nearby Highway 67. Whatever you believe, you may not see anything at all—the lights are apparently very unpredictable.

If you CHOSE THAT:⬇

Be on high alert for the Mackenzie POLTERGEIST when you visit GREYFRIARS CEMETERY in Edinburgh, Scotland. The ghost of Sir George Mackenzie—a town leader who tortured religious rebels in the 17th century—is said to haunt a tomb known as the "BLACK MAUSOLEUM." Visitors frequently report strange sounds and smells coming from the lair, and hundreds have suffered mysterious scratches and burns. Some speculate that a man wandered into the tomb in the 1990s and accidentally awakened Mackenzie's SPIRIT, and he has been upset about it ever since.

THIS:

Search for stolen works of art.

or

THAT:

Search for stolen crown jewels.

MUSE BEFORE YOU CHOOSE Whether you choose masterpieces or treasure, you're still getting a finder's fee!

If you CHOSE ⬇THIS:

You'll be doing a good deed (and probably getting a reward for it) if you discover one of the **MISSING ARTWORKS** from the Nazi plunder during World War II. As Germany conquered much of Western Europe in the 1940s, the Nazis **LOOTED** more than 650,000 masterpieces from private collections and **MUSEUMS.** Although many pieces have been recovered, there are still thousands left unaccounted for or believed to be destroyed. In 2012 more than 1,200 **STOLEN** artworks were discovered in an apartment in Munich, Germany. So keep an eye out if you see a beautiful painting at somebody's yard sale!

Choice Nugget

The Monuments Men were a group of about 345 men and women whose job was to protect Europe's cultural treasures from the destruction of World War II.

If you CHOSE ⬇THAT:

You'll have to think like a detective if you want to find the missing **CROWN JEWELS OF IRELAND.** The jewels went missing from Dublin Castle on July 6, 1907, and they consisted of a collection of ornaments worn on ceremonial occasions by the Order of St. Patrick, a special society loyal to the government. They had been stored in a safe in the castle library that required **TWO KEYS** to open, both of which were in the possession of the castle's manager, Sir Arthur Vicars. After a messenger discovered the jewels had been **STOLEN,** a major investigation was under way. Vicars claimed he was innocent, and no other suspects were ever apprehended. The jewels remain missing to this day.

CHOOSE THIS:

Your mind can "step outside" your body.

or

CHOOSE THAT:

Your ears can detect a strange noise few people can hear.

MUSE BEFORE YOU CHOOSE

What if your mind floats away? What if you can't get the noise out of your head?

If you CHOSE THIS:

You better not be afraid of heights if you are able to have **OUT-OF-BODY EXPERIENCES.** One of these events is described as a sensation of floating outside your body and being able to see yourself from above. In 2014, a Canadian woman claimed to be able to have out-of-body experiences whenever she wanted. She said that she first noticed it when she was a little girl and thought everyone could do it. Researchers at the University of Ottawa found that, as she was experiencing the **FLOATING** sensation, her brain showed activity similar to that seen in high-level athletes who can imagine themselves winning a competition.

If you CHOSE THAT:

You may have a hard time sleeping if you hear the "**TAOS HUM,**" a bizarre sound heard occasionally in north-central New Mexico, U.S.A. First reported in the 1990s, the **LOW-FREQUENCY SOUND** is described as the **WHIR** or **BUZZ** of an idling engine and has no apparent source. What's more mysterious is that only a small percentage of residents can hear the sound. Some say the noise could be spontaneous **OTOACOUSTIC** emissions, or sounds that are generated within the ear itself. People who are more sensitive to sound—and not as surrounded by electronics, traffic, and other noisy distractions—can detect these noises within their ears. But some people remain skeptical about this explanation, mainly because there have been many reports of other **SUSPICIOUS** "hums" around the world, especially in Scotland and England. You'll have to listen very carefully if you want to get to the bottom of *this* mystery!

THIS:

Figure out the solution to a modern **puzzle** for **bragging** rights.

or

CHOOSE

THAT:

scholar Dr. Frank Cross, Jr., studying the Dead Sea Scrolls

Decipher **clues** in an **ancient** riddle for possible **treasure.**

MUSE BEFORE YOU CHOOSE   Think like a CIA agent. Think like Indiana Jones.

If you CHOSE
⬇THIS:

You'll probably rack your brain trying to find the solution to the puzzling **"KRYPTOS"** sculpture encrypted by former **CIA** chairman Edward Scheidt. The S-shaped **SCULPTURE**—located at the Central Intelligence Agency's headquarters in Langley, Virginia, U.S.A.—contains four sections of **ENCRYPTED MESSAGES.** Three of the four puzzles have been decoded, but despite the efforts of the best code-breakers, the last section remains **UNSOLVED.** Crack the code and you might get recruited by the CIA!

◄ "Kryptos" sculpture on the grounds of the CIA headquarters, Langley, Virginia

If you CHOSE
⬇THAT:

▲ Dead Sea copper scroll

Follow the clues on a 2,000-year-old copper scroll and you may find buried gold and silver. Discovered in a cave at **KHIRBET QUMRAN** in Palestine, the copper scroll was among the Dead Sea Scrolls, a set of ancient documents that include the earliest **BIBLICAL TEXTS.** Most of the scrolls were written on parchment or papyrus, so the fact that some scrolls were written on copper meant they contained valuable information that needed to withstand the tests of time. This **COPPER SCROLL** gives the locations of many sites where treasure is possibly buried. Unfortunately, none of the sites described have been found, partly because the locations mentioned in the scroll reference very specific places within cities that no longer exist and partly because we haven't yet deciphered the entire scroll.

ANALYZE
THIS!

If you mostly picked **CHOOSE THIS,** you're a true problem solver who enjoys the process of figuring things out. When you're faced with a puzzle or some strange phenomena, the logical part of your brain goes into hyper-drive. Psychologists refer to your style as solution-focused thinking, which happens to be better than emotion-focused thinking when making tough choices. The only downside to how your brain works is you get so wrapped up in work that you may neglect other people and their feelings. Make sure to develop that side of your personality too by practicing empathy.

ANALYZE
THAT!

If you mostly picked **CHOOSE THAT,** you're some-one who enjoys taking risks that could yield big rewards. Someone else in your family is probably a risk taker too. Your personality makes you exciting to hang out with because you're up for anything and you're always finding fun things to do. The possible downside of this personality is that you might always be chasing the next big thing, which might make it hard for your friends to keep up. Try taking smaller risks for more consistent rewards.

CHAPTER 4

GROSS GUTS

From body odor to frozen heads, this chapter is all about our insides and outsides. Gross? Definitely. But also pretty cool. So dive in and get to know what your insides are all about!

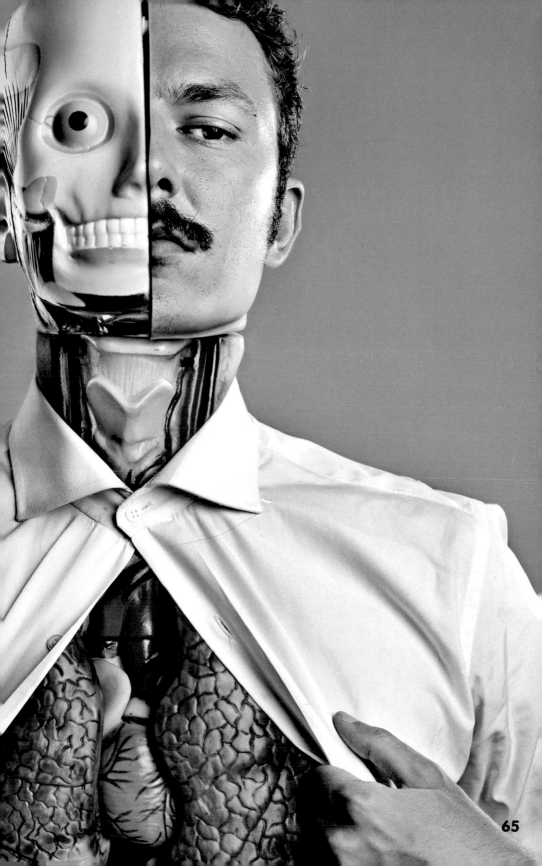

CHOOSE

THIS:

Have **nerves** of **steel.**

or

CHOOSE

THAT:

Have **skin** that **talks** to **you.**

bionic skin ▶

Strength of Superman. Chatty epidermis.

If you CHOSE ⬇THIS:

It takes a lot to be brave, but if you want real **NERVES OF STEEL** you have to go to China. Scientists in China have used liquid metal to help repair severed nerves in **FROGS.** The alloy allows a frog's body to continue signaling between its brain and its muscles, helping to prevent muscle loss. The metal nerves are not really made of steel, but a metal solution made of a gallium-indium-selenium alloy that **STAYS LIQUID** at body temperature. The liquid has bridged severed sciatic nerves from the calf muscles of bullfrogs. The solution allows time for the nerve endings to **GROW BACK SLOWLY** without muscle loss. One day it may help people get out of their wheelchairs and **WALK!**

If you CHOSE ⬇THAT:

Imagine shaking hands with a **ROBOT** and instantly it would know your **TEMPERATURE** and **HEARTBEAT.** Now scientists are taking it one step further by attempting to apply a thin layer of **SMART SKIN** directly to humans. This fabricated skin can possibly be integrated inside our bodies or on the outside. The applications are endless. Perhaps one day a smart skin will be attached to a person just like a temporary tattoo and could **WARN** someone of oncoming problems!

Think Twice!

Will our mechanical creations one day seem as alive as we are? Now that's something to think twice about!

VocaListener singing android

CHOOSE THIS:

Smell feet and armpits all day.

or

CHOOSE THAT:

Have brain surgery without painkillers.

MUSE
BEFORE YOU
CHOOSE

Stinky? Ouch!

If you CHOSE THIS:

There are as many as 3,000 **SWEAT GLANDS** on each square inch (6.5 sq cm) of your feet. The sweat that pours out of them during the day gets trapped in your socks and shoes with odor-causing bacteria. If you work in one of **DR. SCHOLL'S** testing laboratories, you could have the actual job of performing **SMELL TESTS** on **FEET** and **ARMPITS**. If you don't mind the smell of body odor, this might be the perfect job for you. Talk about a job that really stinks!

IN ONE DAY!!

If you CHOSE THAT:

No one wants to think about having **BRAIN SURGERY**, but this might just put your mind a little more at ease. The brain has no **PAIN** receptors, which is why patients can undergo brain surgery while they are still awake, an operation called "awake brain surgery." You are under **ANESTHESIA** during the beginning and end of the procedure, when the doctors remove and reattach your scalp, but patients are awake during the actual surgery. Talk about having a lot on your mind!

If you CHOSE ⬇THIS:

If you like **STRANGE SCIENCE,** a visit to the Complutense University School of Medicine in Madrid, Spain, might be just the thing for you. In the 18th century, a woman was about to give birth when she was struck by a carriage and died outside the hospital. Surgeons took that as an opportunity to **PRESERVE HER IN WAX**—for science! They covered her body in mud to create a mold and filled the mold with wax. The resulting sculpture is still on display at the university!

If you CHOSE ⬇THAT:

If you don't mind the possibility of living long after everyone around you is gone, **CRYOPRESERVATION** might be a great option. Kim Suozzi decided to put herself in the hands of future scientists when she died in 2013 from brain cancer. Upon her death she had her head surgically removed and frozen until a **CURE** is found for her cancer. Cryopreservation, a technique that began in the pages of a science fiction story, is now reality. There are over 200 people, including baseball legend Ted Williams, **FROZEN** in the United States, and another 2,000 have signed up for it!

CHOOSE THIS:

Have **sound waves** aimed at **you.**

or

CHOOSE THAT:

Have **shock** waves **aimed** at **you.**

MUSE
BEFORE YOU
CHOOSE

A concert in your body. An earthquake in your body.

If you CHOSE
↓THIS:

This doesn't mean music! We can't hear these sound waves. Their frequency is TOO LOW for our ears. It's a technology, called MIST, that is being used to speed the healing of wounds. It involves spraying a saline solution over the wound and focusing the SOUND WAVES on the solution. Scientists found that 69 percent of the patients with hard-to-heal wounds were completely healed. Talk about good vibrations!

If you CHOSE
↓THAT:

Roughly 1 in every 11 Americans suffers from small deposits of calcium called KIDNEY STONES. If you ever do get kidney stones, doctors may use shock wave therapy to get rid of them. Doctors have been using the noninvasive shock waves to SHATTER stones inside kidneys for a long time, but now they can pinpoint the stones better with a slight adjustment to the lens that focuses the shock waves. It's like a MINI-EARTHQUAKE in your body!

BEFORE

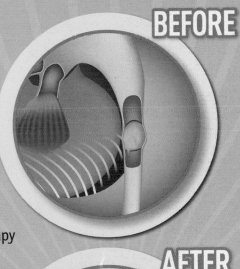

AFTER

73

CHOOSE
THIS:
Put your **urine** to use.

or

CHOOSE
THAT:
Drink **herbal tea.**

MUSE
BEFORE YOU
CHOOSE

Coffee, tea, or pee?

If you CHOSE THIS: ⬇

You might think that if you were stranded on a deserted island with nothing to drink that your **URINE** would be a healthy option. **WRONG!** Urine is not sterile, like many people think. It's 95 percent water, but the extra 5 percent isn't good for you. It contains **BACTERIA** and **URIC ACID** from your kidneys that have been flushed out. Drinking your own urine puts toxins back in your body. That doesn't stop people who claim urine has **HEALING PROPERTIES** and use it to fight cancer or to moisturize their face.

If you CHOSE ⬇THAT:

If you hate the itch of **MOSQUITO BITES**, just think of how horrible it would be to live with the fear of that bite giving you the deadly disease of malaria. Worldwide, 300 million to 500 million people are infected with malaria each year, with most of the cases in sub-Saharan Africa. Thin, gauzy mosquito netting helps keep **MALARIA-CARRYING** mosquitoes at bay, and there are some drugs that can also aid in prevention. The world's most effective antimalarial drug comes from a plant called **SWEET WORMWOOD** that has been used by Chinese doctors for roughly 2,000 years. Today, **TEA** from this plant is used to help with malaria treatment and prevention. There is no quick fix though. It's important to wear long sleeves and pants, and to use mosquito netting in places where malaria is a risk.

CHOOSE **THIS:**

Have endless **flatulence.**

or

CHOOSE **THAT:**

Have endless hiccups.

MUSE BEFORE YOU CHOOSE Ability to clear a room. Peace only when you sleep.

If you CHOSE ⬇THIS:

FLATULENCE, the polite word for passing gas, can be embarrassing. But before you point fingers, you should remember that you do it too. It's caused by foods being broken down during **DIGESTION**. The many bacteria in your gut produce gas as they metabolize the food you eat. And it doesn't happen just to people. Some U.S. politicians are planning to reduce **COW** flatulence as a way to combat global warming. Cow flatulence releases a lot of the greenhouse gas **METHANE**.

Choice Nugget

Most people know that beans are one of the most common gas-producing foods, but did you know that bran, broccoli, and cabbage are also common culprits? Fatty and fried foods can also wreak a gassy havoc.

If you CHOSE ⬇THAT:

Imagine having **HICCUPS** for **60 YEARS**. Having nonstop hiccups is pretty rare, but it does happen. Because of a **BRAIN INJURY**, a man in Iowa, U.S.A., suffered for 60 years, and a girl in Florida, U.S.A., couldn't shake hers for nearly six weeks. The fourth- and fifth-century B.C. Greek physician Hippocrates believed liver inflammation was the culprit, but doctors today can tell you that a hiccup is a spasm of your **DIAPHRAGM** and the muscles between your **RIBS**. The spasm makes you inhale fast and ends with the space near your vocal cords snapping shut.

CHOOSE THIS:

Never cut your nails.

CHOOSE THAT:

Never cut your hair.

MUSE BEFORE YOU CHOOSE

Tough texting. Boundless brushing.

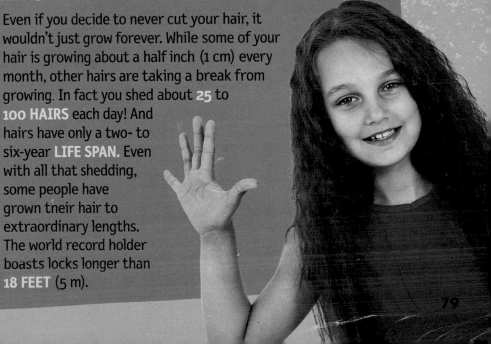

If you CHOSE THIS:

If you decide to take this option, you might end up with nails that can reach **ACROSS THE ROOM.** Nails grow about one-tenth of an inch (3 mm) every month, so you've got to be patient. The world record holder for long nails had fingernails that measured more than **32 FEET** (9.85 m) in combined length. Of course, having tremendously long nails makes using your phone or computer a little difficult, but you could really go to town with a few bottles of nail polish!

If you CHOSE THAT:

Even if you decide to never cut your hair, it wouldn't just grow forever. While some of your hair is growing about a half inch (1 cm) every month, other hairs are taking a break from growing. In fact you shed about **25** to **100 HAIRS** each day! And hairs have only a two- to six-year **LIFE SPAN.** Even with all that shedding, some people have grown their hair to extraordinary lengths. The world record holder boasts locks longer than **18 FEET** (5 m).

ANALYZE
THIS!

If you mostly picked **CHOOSE THIS**, you're the type of person who is not easily grossed out. You laugh in the face of things that make others recoil in disgust. You unflinchingly explore areas where few humans dare to venture. You're probably pretty self-composed and up for anything. You also might be so nonjudgmental because you have a few gross habits yourself! Just ask your friends!

ANALYZE
THAT!

If you mostly picked **CHOOSE THAT**, you've got a personality that is suited to work in the medical field. It takes a lot to work in this area, but one of the most important qualities is the ability to take what some see as bizarre or scary and get valuable information out of it. During my training, I observed a brain surgery on someone who was awake. The procedure was so interesting to me, but incredibly disturbing to many others. You're the type of person with this unique curiosity, so don't let other people stop you just because they're a little queasy.

CHAPTER 5

PARTY TIME!

From Tokyo to New York City, people sure know how to throw a good party! This chapter is all about world festivals and celebrations—some of which you may find a little bizarre!

CHOOSE **THIS:**

Fall into a trance-like **state.**

or

CHOOSE **THAT:**

Hang out with a **witch** doctor.

Peaceful. Nausea. Have your fortune told. Curses.

If you CHOSE ⬇THIS:

You may get dizzy watching performers if you attend MEVLÂNA, a ten-day festival in Konya, Turkey, that is held every December. For over 750 years, a group called the WHIRLING DERVISHES has performed an elegant, trance-like dance that involves spinning in circles for hours. A dervish is a member of a Muslim RELIGIOUS ORDER called the Mevlevi. The spinning ritual is based on the 13th-century writings of Rumi, a philosopher who believed that whirling helped achieve divine harmony. Roughly one million people, mostly from Turkey, attend the festival each year. Now that's a party!

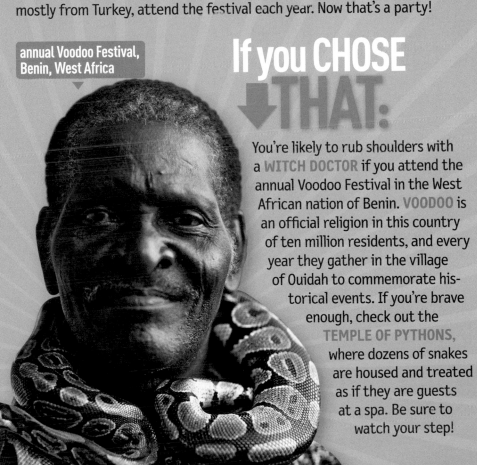

whirling dervishes in Turkey

annual Voodoo Festival, Benin, West Africa

If you CHOSE ⬇THAT:

You're likely to rub shoulders with a WITCH DOCTOR if you attend the annual Voodoo Festival in the West African nation of Benin. VOODOO is an official religion in this country of ten million residents, and every year they gather in the village of Ouidah to commemorate historical events. If you're brave enough, check out the TEMPLE OF PYTHONS, where dozens of snakes are housed and treated as if they are guests at a spa. Be sure to watch your step!

THIS:

Make **mud pies** **with** your **friends.**

or

THAT:

Squirt water guns at **strangers.**

MUSE BEFORE YOU CHOOSE Dirty fingernails. Ruin your clothes. Splash fights. Cool off.

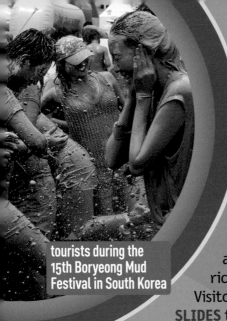

tourists during the 15th Boryeong Mud Festival in South Korea

If you CHOSE ⬇THIS:

You can count on getting dirty when you show up for the **MUD FESTIVAL** in Boryeong, South Korea. Held every summer since 1998, the celebration began as a way to promote the region's mineral-rich mud, which is used in local **COSMETICS**. Visitors will enjoy everything mud—from **MUD SLIDES** to **MUD SKIING!** Be sure to get dirty right away or else you will be thrown into **MUD "PRISON"**— a jail-like area where spectators throw globs of mud at people who are deemed too clean!

If you CHOSE ⬇THAT:

Be sure to pack your **SUPER SOAKER** when you go to the Songkran water festival held every April in **THAILAND.** Traditionally, people would sprinkle water on each other as a sign of respect and well wishes in the Thai New Year and Buddhist festival, but over time the holiday has become more about having fun and **COOLING OFF** during one of the hottest months. April temperatures can rise above 100°F (38°C), so partygoers relieve the heat by having a countrywide water war. Tourists are especially vulnerable to getting attacked by swarms of local kids with water guns, so be prepared for a splashing good time!

CHOOSE **THIS:**

Take a ride **in a** coffin, **but** you are **not dead.**

or

CHOOSE **THAT:**

Sprint through **city** streets, **but** you risk **injury** or **death.**

Running of the Bulls

MUSE BEFORE YOU CHOOSE Claustrophobia. Live to see another day. Good exercise. Possible death.

If you CHOSE ↓THIS:

You're in for one weird memory if you decide to go to **FROZEN DEAD GUY DAYS**, an annual celebration held in Nederland, Colorado, U.S.A. Coffin racing, ice turkey bowling, and brain freeze contests are some of the scheduled activities that are meant to commemorate a day in the mid-1990s when **BREDO MORSTOEL'S** body was found frozen in a shack behind his daughter's house. No, his death didn't involve a **CRIME**—he had asked his family members to **PRESERVE HIS BODY** until modern technology was advanced enough to bring him back to life. The discovery caused quite a stir in the small Colorado town. Nowadays, the dead Grandpa Bredo (or so he is called) is honored with a day that—ironically— brings a burst of life to the community.

Frozen Dead Guy Days in Nederland, Colorado, U.S.A.

If you CHOSE ↓THAT:

If going for a brisk jog interests you, perhaps you should raise the stakes by running in front of a **DOZEN BULLS!** The nine-day Festival of San Fermín in Pamplona, Spain, is known for a tradition called the *encierro*, where bulls are set loose in the city streets and thrill seekers must **SPRINT** to avoid getting **TRAMPLED** or **GORED** by horns. It's a dangerous ritual that goes back hundreds of years, but it's actually only one small part of the festival. Over a million partygoers from around the world come to Pamplona to enjoy the parades, fireworks, and shows, making it one of the largest annual **FIESTAS** in Spain.

CHOOSE THIS:

Carefully paint detailed designs on your skin.

MUSE BEFORE YOU CHOOSE

"Living" artwork.
Temporary.
Rainbow fun!
Dusty.

CHOOSE THAT:

Go wild and throw colorful powders on others.

If you CHOSE THIS:

Your flesh will be a work of art if you participate in the **WORLD BODYPAINTING FESTIVAL** in Pörtschach, Austria. Every year, tens of thousands of people are drawn to the spectacle where artists show off their imaginations—on their skin! From **ALIENS** to **FAIRIES**, there's no telling what creatures you'll see. Many hours are spent painstakingly applying layers of paint by hand or airbrush, so you'll need a great deal of **PATIENCE** if you're competing. At the end of the day, the paint is washed off and the creatures are made human again!

If you CHOSE THAT:

Let loose next spring and head to India for the **FESTIVAL OF COLORS**, also known as Holi. It's an ancient Hindu festival that has become increasingly popular in other parts of the world. People use this holiday as a time to end conflicts, to make peace, and to forgive and forget. Celebrations start with a **BONFIRE** where people gather to **SING** and **DANCE**. The next morning participants color each other with **DRY POWDER** and **COLORED WATER**.

people at Holi, the Festival of Colors

CHOOSE THIS:

Keep both feet on the ground.

or

CHOOSE THAT:

Spread your wings and fly.

Albuquerque International Balloon Fiesta

MUSE BEFORE YOU CHOOSE

Play it safe. Live on the edge. Vertigo.

If you CHOSE ↓ THIS:

No need to fret about heights next November if you show up for the **MACY'S THANKSGIVING DAY PARADE** in New York City. You and an estimated three million spectators will gather in the streets to watch the famous giant balloons float along a 2.5-mile (4-km) course. It takes about 90 minutes to fill one of the balloons with a mixture of helium and air, and then they are covered in nets so they don't float away. Started in 1924, the Thanksgiving Day Parade is now viewed by some **50 MILLION** people on television—so be sure to wave to the cameras!

Macy's Thanksgiving Day Parade

If you CHOSE THAT: ↓

You'll soar like an eagle if you participate in the **ALBUQUERQUE INTERNATIONAL BALLOON FIESTA** held in New Mexico, U.S.A., every October. This nine-day event features more than 500 balloons, making it the largest hot air balloon festival in the world. The event began in 1972 as a 50th birthday celebration for a local radio station. You and other balloon enthusiasts will get the rare opportunity to see the balloons inflated on the launch field and take off in two mass waves, filling the sky with balloons all at once. Launch directors—called "zebras" because of their black-and-white uniforms—serve as traffic cops to make sure all the balloons take off safely. The balloons come in all shapes and sizes—from **BARNYARD ANIMALS** to **PLANETS**. Even Darth Vader has made an appearance at the fiesta!

Think Twice!

A "balloonicle" is a giant balloon that can be driven around a parade like a vehicle.

CHOOSE

THIS:

Watch a building go **up** in **ice.**

or

CHOOSE

THAT:

Watch a **ship** go **down** in **flames.**

MUSE BEFORE YOU CHOOSE

Impressive igloos. Cold construction.
Roast marshmallows. Toasty warm.

If you CHOSE ⬇THIS:

If **ICE SCULPTURES** are your thing, you're sure to be impressed by the Harbin Ice and Snow Festival in northern China. This monthlong winter celebration features massive ice sculptures that are carved to look like famous structures, like the Eiffel Tower. Here, you and a million other visitors will take part in all things **COLD**—from **SKIING** to **SLEDDING** to racing down a 787-foot-tall (240-m) **ICE SLIDE!**

Harbin Ice and Snow Festival

If you CHOSE THAT:⬇

It will be a **BONFIRE** you'll never forget at the Up Helly Aa, a winter festival held in the remote Shetland Islands of Scotland. After nightfall hundreds of men dressed in **VIKING** costumes parade through the streets waving torches in the air as they make their way to a reproduction of a **LONGSHIP** they built over four months. The "Vikings" sing a traditional song and then launch their torches onto the ship!

Up Helly Aa fire festival

Think Twice!

Ice lanterns are a winter tradition going back to the 1600s.

1. Water is poured into a bucket and allowed to freeze.

2. The bucket is gently warmed so the block of ice can be removed and its center chiseled out.

3. A candle is placed inside, resulting in a windproof lantern.

CHOOSE THIS:

Stop and smell the roses.

or

CHOOSE THAT:

Find yourself in a massive food fight.

MUSE BEFORE YOU CHOOSE

Sweet scents. Beautiful colors. Tasty fun. Sticky skin.

If you CHOSE THIS:

Your nose will thank you when you attend the **ROSE FESTIVAL** in Morocco. In spring, a region near the High Atlas Mountains is colored a vibrant pink, as the Persian roses are in full bloom. The flowers are harvested mid-May for the sweet-smelling festival, which draws about **20,000 PEOPLE.** It's a three-day celebration of the crops and the beauty of nature, filled with **SONG** and **DANCE, FEASTS,** and a **CHARIOT** procession through a shower of rose petals. You'll even see the petals transported to the local factories where their oils are extracted to produce rose water, a scented liquid used in cooking and perfumes.

If you CHOSE THAT:

Don't wear your fanciest clothes when you show up for **LA TOMATINA,** a festival held every August in **BUÑOL, SPAIN,** where participants throw crushed tomatoes for the sheer fun of it. The celebration begins with the *palo jabón,* an activity that involves climbing a slippery pole with a ham on top. Once someone is able to drop the ham from the pole, a signal is given that the tomato fight is to begin! Over **150,000 TOMATOES** are crushed and then launched into the air for one entire hour. You may want to consider wearing goggles to this massive tomato toss!

Think Twice!

Ivrea, Italy, is known for its annual Battle of the Oranges, a large food fight in which nearly a half million pounds (226,000 kg) of oranges are thrown as part of a reenactment of an ancient battle.

ANALYZE
THIS!

If you mostly picked **CHOOSE THIS,** you're the type of person who loves to be a spectator and observe the world around you. In your mind, partying is more about relaxing and cheering on someone else. This probably makes you an excellent friend. The good news is there is little risk involved when you have this type of personality. However, sometimes it's good to step outside your comfort zone and try getting into the game!

ANALYZE
THAT!

If you mostly picked **CHOOSE THAT,** you're the type of person who likes to take the bull by the horns—literally! To you, it's not a party unless you're totally lost in the moment. Psychologists call this a feeling of flow, and it happens when we get really engaged in a fun or meaningful activity. You're probably also a bit of a risk taker. Just remember, keep a clear mind and pay attention to your surroundings, even when you're going with the flow!

CHAPTER 6

WIN
or
LOSE

Choose between these exciting competitions. Win or lose, these challenges will leave you speechless, stuffed, or just plain exhausted.

CHOOSE THIS:

Dance your feet off.

CHOOSE THAT:

MUSE BEFORE YOU CHOOSE

Holes in your shoes. Sore throat.

Sing your heart out.

If you CHOSE THIS:

If you've ever wished you could dance with the stars, then the USA Dance National **DANCESPORT CHAMPIONSHIPS** are for you. But be prepared to come up against some pretty stiff competition. Nine-year-old Jhailyn Farcon and ten-year-old Joshua Ginzburg are serious **BALLROOM DANCE** contenders even though they practice in separate states. Jhailyn lives in New Jersey and Joshua lives in Massachusetts, making their onstage presence even more magical! They've mastered the **JIVE, CHA CHA, RUMBA,** and **SAMBA.** The two placed third at the national dance championships in one category.

Choice Nugget

The a cappella tournament was featured in the 2012 movie *Pitch Perfect*, starring Anna Kendrick, Brittany Snow, and Rebel Wilson.

If you CHOSE THAT:

Hey, who needs a band when you can **CREATE YOUR OWN** music? If consistently hitting pitch-perfect high notes is your thing, then the International Championship of Collegiate A Cappella is your competition. Called the NCAA Championships for **A CAPPELLA,** this competition brings together the best groups from colleges and high schools around the world.

CHOOSE **THIS:**

Eat **141** hard-**boiled** eggs in **8** minutes.

or

CHOOSE **THAT:**

Eat **72 cupcakes** in 6 **minutes.**

MUSE
BEFORE YOU
CHOOSE

Funky odors. Sugar rush.

If you CHOSE
⬇THIS:

You might like decorating eggs to celebrate Easter, but this is about eating them! We're not talking deviled eggs or egg salad; this is straight up, out-of-the-shell, hard-boiled. **JOEY CHESTNUT** managed to gobble up 141 in a record 8 minutes in 2013. That wasn't the first time Joey conquered a **FOOD CHALLENGE**. He's won over 30! He's also stepped up to the plate to eat more than 4 apple pies in 8 minutes and 118 jalapeño poppers in just 10 minutes. Maybe he isn't the person to **INVITE** to your next barbecue!

If you CHOSE THAT:⬇

You might want to take on this **SWEET** challenge, but think again. That's a lot of cupcakes! Not a problem for **PATRICK BERTOLETTI**, who holds more world records in eating than anyone, including devouring 42 PB&J sandwiches in 10 minutes. The one championship he **HASN'T WON** is the Nathan's Hot Dog Eating Contest. Imagine sitting between Patrick and Joey Chestnut at the next contest. No way!

Choice Nugget

Major League Eating oversees all professional eating contests. Check out their events, but don't watch on a full stomach!

CHOOSE

THIS:

Cheer your way to a **win**.

or

CHOOSE

THAT:

Play your **music** on the **field**.

MUSE BEFORE YOU CHOOSE Pom-poms. No music stands.

If you CHOSE ⬇THIS:

Whether you prefer your game on the **FIELD** or on the **SIDELINES,** this competition is a great choice. The National High School Cheerleading Championship is the place where **CHEERLEADERS** can compete against other cheerleaders for the big prize. If you don't think cheerleading is a **SPORT,** tell that to the competitors, who practice countless hours on dance and **GYMNASTIC** moves to create winning routines. So grab those sneakers and get your cheer on!

If you CHOSE ⬇THAT:

If you can master more than one thing at a time, then entering a **MARCHING BAND** competition is a great choice. Not only do you have to be able to play your instrument as you march in formation, you have to be able to entertain a crowd with precision **CHOREOGRAPHY.** And don't forget this isn't all about trumpets and drums; it also includes flag twirlers and dancers. A marching band brings as much excitement to a field as the **FOOTBALL** players. So pick up that instrument and get marching!

CHOOSE THIS:

Invent the next big thing.

or

CHOOSE THAT:

Spell your way to the finish.

MUSE BEFORE YOU CHOOSE Problem solver. Dictionary overload.

If you CHOSE ⬇THIS:

Are you the next Albert Einstein? You might just end up inducted into the National Gallery for **AMERICA'S YOUNG INVENTORS.** To enter, you need to be either a national invention competition winner or a patent holder, or already have your product on the market. If any of these things applies to you, you could be eligible to be part of this prestigious Hall of Fame, like Meredith Barr, who invented a biodiesel processor that doubles the energy efficiency of **BIODIESEL** production.

If you CHOSE THAT:⬇

Are you an ace at your spelling tests? Then check out your local **SPELLING BEE.** With any luck you might just end up at the Scripps National Spelling Bee like 2014 champions Sriram Hathwar and Ansun Sujoe. For the first time in 52 years, the spelling bee had two spellers tie for **FIRST PLACE!** After both boys spelled a dozen words correctly in a row, the two were declared co-champions!

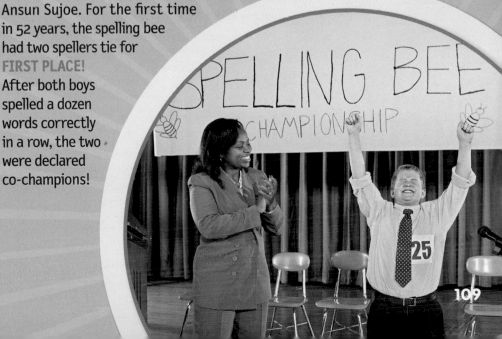

109

THIS:

Solve your **way** to the **championships.**

or

THAT:

Build your **win** one **letter** at a **time.**

MUSE BEFORE YOU CHOOSE Think out of the box. Place tiles in the box.

If you CHOSE ↓THIS:

If you enjoy building with LEGOS, this challenging contest is for you. Over 230,000 kids from ages roughly 9 to 16 from over 70 countries compete in the First Lego League (FLL) World Class Challenge. Each challenge is divided into three parts: the ROBOT GAME, the PROJECT, and the First Lego League CORE VALUES. Teams of up to ten kids and one coach develop a solution to a problem in each category. It's not all about Legos. Teams explore NANOTECHNOLOGY, climate change, and other topics. The theme for 2013 was "Nature's Fury." Who knows what challenges future teams will face?

If you CHOSE ↓THAT:

Take on the SCRABBLE challenge with this national competition. The North American Scrabble Players Association sponsors a high-energy tournament every year for people of all skill levels. The 2014 National School Scrabble champions appeared on *Jimmy Kimmel Live!* This level of competition is open to students in GRADES 4–8 in the U.S.A. and Canada, and the winning two-player team receives a cash PRIZE. Not bad for playing a game!

CHOOSE THIS:

Save the planet.

CHOOSE THAT:

Investigate the past.

MUSE BEFORE YOU CHOOSE

Outdoors in the field. Inside in the stacks.

If you CHOSE THIS:

If you are attempting a superhero lifestyle, try competing in the **NORTH AMERICAN ENVIROTHON.** It will get you geared up for conquering the big problems facing the environment. Winning teams from high schools in the United States and Canada compete for recognition and scholarships. Each competition focuses on a current environmental issue, such as urban pollution, invasive species and their effect on biodiversity, agriculture land conservation, and managing natural **RESOURCES.**

If you CHOSE THAT:

They say that you need to study the past so that you don't repeat it. If you are a history wiz, the **NATIONAL HISTORY DAY** competition might be right up your alley. You, along with more than a half million other kids, will choose a historical topic and conduct your own **RESEARCH.** You'll get to peruse museums, archives, and libraries. You'll conduct oral history interviews and get to visit historic sites. And after you present your findings, you get a prize!

Kids participate in the National History Day competition.

CHOOSE

THIS:

Create a masterpiece to end **poverty**.

or

CHOOSE

THAT:

Write a best-selling **novel**.

MUSE BEFORE YOU CHOOSE Pick up a brush. Pick up a pen.

If you CHOSE THIS: ⬇

This is all about art and **FIGHTING POVERTY.** Can the two go hand in hand? The United Nations thought so. Over 12,000 kids from all over the world created **ART** themed on ending poverty in the International Children's Art Competition. They depicted cooperation, fairness, unity, compassion, and solidarity. Six winning designs were issued as **UN STAMPS** in 2008. Every year since 1991 the UN has sponsored the contest with a different theme. In 2013 the theme was food waste. Become an activist with your art!

If you CHOSE ⬇THAT:

The annual Junior Authors Short Story Writing Contest is the perfect contest for **BUDDING AUTHORS.** Put your pen to paper or your fingers to your keyboard to craft a unique short story. The contest is open to writers ages 9–21 in all countries, but the story must be written in English. This is just one of many writing contests offered to **STORYTELLERS.** Who knows, you might just be the next Rick Riordan or Kate DiCamillo!

LET'S SEE WHAT **YOUR CHOICES** SAY **ABOUT YOU.**

DOC TALK ...

PSYCHOLOGIST **DR. MATT BELLACE** DISSECTS YOUR **DECISIONS ...**

ANALYZE
THIS!

If you mostly picked **CHOOSE THIS,** you're definitely a hands-on type of person who is willing to go all in for a competition. Psychologists have learned that competing successfully in anything requires confidence in your abilities and even self-deception. Believing in yourself whether you're the best or not is just as important as having a high level of skill. Committing your mind and body to winning turns out to be the best recipe for achievement. Even if you lose, just think of all the fun you'll have and friends you'll meet along the way!

ANALYZE
THAT!

If you mostly picked **CHOOSE THAT,** verbal abilities are definitely one of your strengths! Whether you're spelling accurately, singing with passion, or eating really fast, you use your mouth like a pitcher uses his arm. As someone who speaks and writes for a living, I'm happy to report that language ability gets better with age! Just remember, if you don't use it, you lose it. The human brain only strengthens connections that are used regularly. Try keeping a journal and keep reading lots and lots of books!

CHAPTER **7**

SILLY

STATS

Ever wonder how many stacked hamsters it would take to reach the top of the Statue of Liberty? Well, that makes you one curious (and strange) kid! This chapter is all about some numbers that are just downright silly.

giant floating rubber duck sculpture

THIS:
See **100 elephants** floating in the **air.**

or

THAT:
See **140 ants** floating in the **air.**

**MUSE
BEFORE YOU
CHOOSE** Flying stampedes. Falling poop. Airborne insects. Suspended colonies.

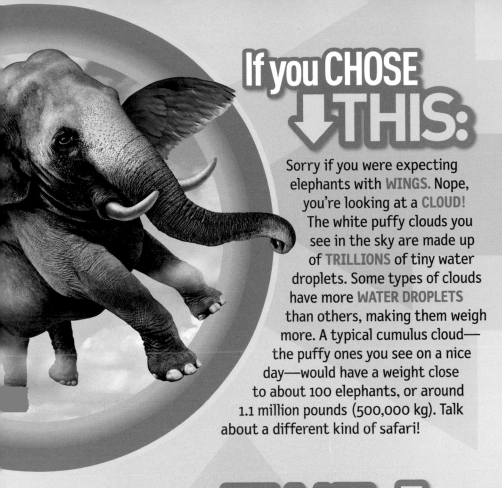

If you CHOSE ⬇THIS:

Sorry if you were expecting elephants with WINGS. Nope, you're looking at a CLOUD! The white puffy clouds you see in the sky are made up of TRILLIONS of tiny water droplets. Some types of clouds have more WATER DROPLETS than others, making them weigh more. A typical cumulus cloud—the puffy ones you see on a nice day—would have a weight close to about 100 elephants, or around 1.1 million pounds (500,000 kg). Talk about a different kind of safari!

If you CHOSE THAT:⬇

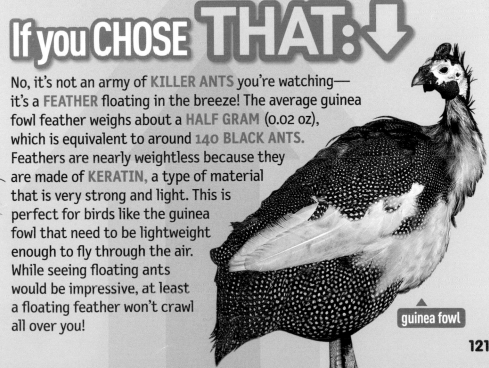

No, it's not an army of KILLER ANTS you're watching—it's a FEATHER floating in the breeze! The average guinea fowl feather weighs about a HALF GRAM (0.02 oz), which is equivalent to around 140 BLACK ANTS. Feathers are nearly weightless because they are made of KERATIN, a type of material that is very strong and light. This is perfect for birds like the guinea fowl that need to be lightweight enough to fly through the air. While seeing floating ants would be impressive, at least a floating feather won't crawl all over you!

guinea fowl

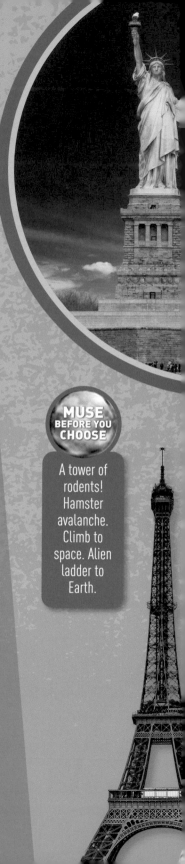

CHOOSE
THIS:

Stack hamsters to the height of a famous monument.

CHOOSE
THAT:

Stack monuments all the way to the moon's surface.

MUSE BEFORE YOU CHOOSE

A tower of rodents! Hamster avalanche. Climb to space. Alien ladder to Earth.

If you CHOSE THIS:

You've got quite a **BALANCING ACT** if you try to stack **HAMSTERS** to the top of the Statue of Liberty in New York City. The height of the monument—from base to torch—is about 151 feet (46 m). The average height of a hamster standing on its hind legs is **SIX INCHES** (15 cm). That means if you created a tower of hamsters that reached the top of Lady Liberty, you'd need **302** in all! It would stink to be the hamster on the bottom, wouldn't it?

If you CHOSE THAT:

You're reaching for the stars if you try to get to the moon by stacking **EIFFEL TOWERS** on top of each other. The height of the Eiffel Tower in Paris, France, is **986 FEET** (301 m). The distance from the Earth's surface to the **MOON** at its closest is about **223,700 MILES** (360,000 km). If you were to stack Eiffel Tower upon Eiffel Tower all the way to the moon, it would require more than **1.1 MILLION** monuments! Be sure to build an elevator while you're at it.

Choice Nugget

If you lined up 45 crocodiles tail to snout they would stretch as long as one side of the Great Pyramid of Giza.

THIS:

Eat a dog made out of cheese.

or

CHOOSE

THAT:

Drink a trash can full of milk.

MUSE BEFORE YOU CHOOSE

Cheddar Chihuahuas. Gouda schnauzers. Smelly dairy. Milk overdose.

If you CHOSE ⬇THIS:

Pass the NACHO-CHEESY ... canine? According to a 2013 study on American diets, the average person eats about 23 POUNDS (10.4 kg) of cheese every year. That's roughly the weight of a COCKER SPANIEL! We're eating three times more cheese than in 1970, when the average was 8 pounds (3.5 kg), or more than the weight of the average Chihuahua. That's not good news for our HEALTH since cheese can contain quite a bit of fat. Wonder what will happen if the trend continues and we start eating cheesy Great Danes?

baby hippos

If you CHOSE THAT:⬇

On average, Americans drink 13 GALLONS (49 L) of milk every year, or roughly the amount that would fill a standard kitchen trash can. Perhaps you thought that number would be higher? Back in 1970, Americans drank about 21 gallons (80 L) of milk, which is about how much water you use in the shower. Researchers suspect that this DOWNWARD TREND may be due to the larger selection of beverages we have to choose from than we had in the 1970s. Even though some kinds of milk have a lot of fat, they are healthier for us than sodas!

CHOOSE THIS:

Have some smelly dreams.

or

CHOOSE THAT:

Have some smelly breath.

MUSE BEFORE YOU CHOOSE

Stinky sleep. Restful aromas. Foul fumes. Reeking exhales.

If you CHOSE ⬇THIS:

You're not having a night-mare—you're just PASS-ING GAS! Whether you'd like to admit it or not, the average person toots about 14 TIMES A DAY. Some of these you may be willing to own up to, but others you won't even know have escaped! Most flatulence takes place AT NIGHT while we're sleeping, when we're nice and relaxed and don't have to worry about causing a scene. It is caused by gases trapped in your DIGESTIVE TRACT—and it's a completely natural part of digestion. So if you let out a stinker in your sleep and it wakes you up, don't worry about it!

If you CHOSE THAT: ⬇

You might want to pop a peppermint! Some researchers have estimated that about six in ten Americans have bad breath. People who always have bad breath are said to have CHRONIC HALITOSIS. These oral fumes are usually caused by the bacteria collecting on food remaining in the mouth—on teeth, gums, and the tongue. The BACTERIA release a SULFUR GAS that gives your breath a smelly odor. Foods like garlic and onions are known to make the problem worse. DAILY BRUSHING and flossing usually take care of bad breath, but if you find yourself far away from a toothbrush, you can always chew some gum!

127

THIS:

Go to an amusement park that's **covered** in **pizza**.

or

THAT:

Dive **into** a **swimming** **pool** that's filled with **popcorn**.

MUSE BEFORE YOU CHOOSE

Pepperoni roller coasters. Mushroom mascots. Buttery backstrokes. Crunchy cannonballs.

If you CHOSE THIS:↓

You're going to **WALT DISNEY WORLD** ... and it's covered in **PIZZA!** Americans eat 350 slices of pizza every second, or about **100 ACRES** (40.5 ha) of pizza every day. The Disney World resort in Lake Buena Vista, Florida—complete with theme parks and hotels—covers nearly 25,600 acres (10,360 ha). That means that in **LESS THAN A YEAR,** Americans will have eaten a pizza the size of Disney World. Instead of seeing *Pirates of the Caribbean* you'll see *Pirates of the Pepperoni!*

If you CHOSE ↓THAT:

You'd probably need a fire hose to spray butter on a pool filled with **POPCORN!** Americans consume about **17.3 BILLION** quarts of popcorn every year. To put that number into perspective, let's break it down to just one day. In just 24 hours, Americans go through about **18 OLYMPIC-SIZE** swimming pools full of popcorn. Could you imagine diving into all that crunchy goodness? The only thing you'd need is a movie playing on a *very* big screen!

CHOOSE **THIS:**

Give a **ship**-size **chocolate** to your **valentine.**

or

CHOOSE **THAT:**

Give an **airplane**-size **candy** corn to **trick**-or-**treaters.**

MUSE BEFORE YOU CHOOSE

Yummy cabins. Melting in the sun. Edible wings. Dissolving in the rain.

If you CHOSE ↓THIS:

Your **VALENTINE** sweetheart will be super impressed with a chocolate **CRUISE SHIP**! Americans purchase around **58 MILLION POUNDS** (26 million kg) of chocolate in the days leading up to February 14. That number is so big it's hard to imagine how much chocolate that is. Well, if you compare it to the average cruise ship—which can weigh around 70,000 tons (63,500 mT)—it would equal **2.5 SHIPS** made out of **CHOCOLATE!**

Choice Nugget

You know those heart-shaped candies you see on Valentine's Day with cute messages like BE MINE or XOXO? Americans buy around eight billion heart candies between February 1 and February 14!

If you CHOSE ↓THAT:

Your house will be the most popular this Halloween if you hand out **GIANT** candy corns the size of the Airbus A380, the largest passenger jet **EVER BUILT**. Every year, Americans purchase around 20 million pounds (9 million kg) of candy corn, which is the equivalent of **16 JETS!** This aircraft can seat as many as 853 passengers. But before you schedule a test flight on your candy corn plane, keep in mind that flying through water-filled clouds will likely **DISSOLVE** your wings and send you crashing to the ground!

CHOOSE THIS:

Get paid a dollar every time you blink your eyes.

or

CHOOSE THAT:

Lucrative eyeball lubrication. Rewarding respiration.

Get paid two dollars every time you take a breath.

If you CHOSE THIS:

You'd have about **$20** in your pocket after a **MINUTE'S** worth of blinks! The average person blinks between 15 and 20 times a minute, which helps **LUBRICATE** the eyeballs and clear away any dust or dirt. But recent research shows that blinking may also serve a different purpose. A group of Japanese scientists think that briefly closing our eyes helps us process information about the world and allows us to focus our attention. With all the crazy stuff we see every day, **BLINKING** may give us a momentary pause to gather our thoughts. So not only would those 20 bucks from blinking buy you a new video game, they'd also bring you a little peace of mind!

If you CHOSE THAT:

The amount of money you'd make from breathing will depend on how old you are. Babies and young children normally breathe faster than older children and adults. As newborns, we take between **30** and **60 BREATHS PER MINUTE,** which would translate to as much as $120! Doctors say we breathe so fast at this age because we are adjusting to life outside the womb. Our bodies gradually fall into a comfortable breathing pattern, and as we get older, we breathe between 12 and 20 times per minute. Getting paid two bucks a breath would get you as much as **40 DOLLARS** in a **MINUTE,** so that's not too bad!

ANALYZE
THIS!

If you mostly picked **CHOOSE THIS,** you're a warmhearted person who loves animals and comfort foods. These traits make you an ideal friend and a fun companion. Spending time with friendly animals is known to be a natural stress reliever for humans, so you probably have lower stress levels too. The only downside of your style is that comfort foods are often high in fat and sugar. In this respect, moderation is the way to go so you can enjoy cheesy pizza and chocolate for many years to come.

ANALYZE
THAT!

If you mostly picked **CHOOSE THAT,** you're a bit of an outrageous person who likes things supersize. You probably wear oversize clothes, say outlandish things, and listen to music louder than your parents can tolerate. The good news is that everyone knows your name and probably likes you, since people tend to remember extroverted characters in a positive light. Just remember to let other people share in the spotlight too.

CHAPTER 8

GO-GO GADGETS

The world of science fiction comes to life with today's amazing gadgets and sophisticated technology. From smart clothes to 3-D printers, these choices will leave you wondering ... what's next?

CHOOSE **THIS:**

Wear a magic decoder **ring.**

or

CHOOSE **THAT:**

Wave your **hand** to catch a **train.**

Code-breaker. Easy rider.

If you CHOSE ⬇THIS:

If you choose to wear these bracelets and rings, you might be able to UNDERSTAND American Sign Language without any lessons. Designers from Asia University have created rings and bracelets that "read" the MOVEMENTS of sign language and allow them to be transmitted into speech. Your response is transmitted into text, which appears on the BRACELET. American Sign Language, just one of the over 200 sign languages used worldwide, has many nuances, so this invention probably wouldn't replace the role of interpreters, but it could be helpful in breaking down some communication barriers.

If you CHOSE THAT:⬇

If you choose to wear this RING, you can ride the RAILS in Boston, Massachusetts, U.S.A., with just a fist bump. Sesame Rings, developed by MIT and Singapore University of Technology and Design, are 3-D-printed and contain a CHIP that enables wearers to SCAN them at the fare gates without having to purchase a train ticket.

Think Twice!

Could the sign language ring be programmed to translate anything we say or sign? Imagine visiting a foreign country and being understood without ever learning the native language. Good idea?

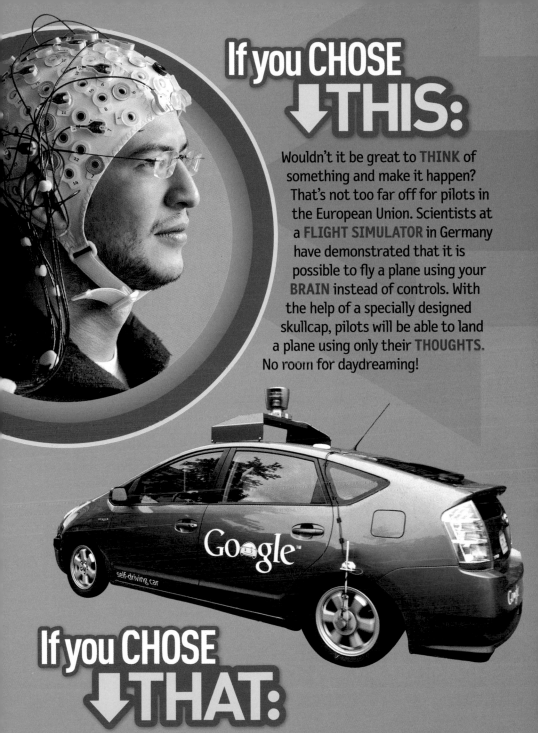

If you CHOSE ⬇THIS:

Wouldn't it be great to **THINK** of something and make it happen? That's not too far off for pilots in the European Union. Scientists at a **FLIGHT SIMULATOR** in Germany have demonstrated that it is possible to fly a plane using your **BRAIN** instead of controls. With the help of a specially designed skullcap, pilots will be able to land a plane using only their **THOUGHTS**. No room for daydreaming!

If you CHOSE ⬇THAT:

SELF-DRIVING CARS might seem like something out of a science fiction movie, but they are fast becoming a reality. Google and other companies have been test-driving self-driving cars that use **GPS** and sensor technology to **NAVIGATE** on their own. Talk about an easy rider!

CHOOSE **THIS:**

Turn your **world** into a **video** game.

or

CHOOSE **THAT:**

Create **any** room **you** can **imagine.**

If you CHOSE ⬇THIS:

You won't worry about running into any walls during your next **VIRTUAL REALITY** gaming session. The Cortex, developed by Sulon Technologies, is a headset with unique sensors that map the world around you. Once you strap on the **HEADSET** your entire world becomes melded with virtual reality. Think of all the possibilities!

If you CHOSE THAT: ⬇

You won't ever have to set up chairs again. The **SPACE GENERATOR** prototype has preprogrammed module cells that can be raised or lowered to **TRANSFORM** the once flat platform into any number of 3-D arrangements. Just think about it. You could transform the space into a theater or fashion show runway or a **MAZE** for gaming with just the touch of a button. This invention leaves much more time for snack planning!

THIS:

Match wits with a computer.

or

THAT:

Have a computer be your maid.

MUSE BEFORE YOU CHOOSE You might lose. Robot assistants.

If you CHOSE ⬇THIS:

You've probably played a virtual **GAME** against a computer at some point. Did you win? Imagine chatting online with a gaming partner and realizing it's **NOT A HUMAN** but a cleverly coded piece of software, or "**CHATBOX**." Supposedly, a chatbox fooled a third of the judges in a chat challenge into thinking it was a 13-year-old boy named Eugene Goostman.

If you CHOSE ⬇THAT:

Computers can help you do a lot of things, but be your own personal assistant? The latest version of **GOOGLE NOW** on Android does. It analyzes trends in your personal habits to bring you **INFORMATION** that is relevant to you. With this new technology you never have to worry about **DOZING OFF** and missing your bus stop. It knows how close you are before you do!

Think Twice!

Could robots or computers replace us? They already have in many manufacturing plants.

CHOOSE THIS:

Get a hug from your hoodie.

or

CHOOSE THAT:

Message friends on the sly.

MUSE BEFORE YOU CHOOSE

Super snug.
Super spy.

If you CHOSE
THIS:

Get a **REMOTE HUG** from your parent, teacher, or friend from anywhere. T.Jacket, with integrated **AIR BAGS**, actually delivers the pressure of a hug on command from a smartphone or tablet app. Everyone could use a hug!

If you CHOSE
THAT:

A **SMART HOODIE** was developed by New York University grad students. They've basically integrated a **CELL PHONE** into a hooded sweatshirt that would enable you to cover your head and send a text message or roll up your sleeve to post on Facebook. This can be neat and discreet, but be careful about throwing the hoodie in the washing machine!

THIS:

Grow more arms.

or

THAT:

Ditch your glasses.

MUSE BEFORE YOU CHOOSE More arms, more work. Clear eyes, clear skies.

If you CHOSE THIS: ⬇

Have you ever wished you had an **EXTRA ARM** to catch a baseball during a game? Supernumerary robotic technology adds to the abilities we're given at birth to do just that. This recent invention makes Spider-Man's Doctor Octopus a reality. Researchers have developed additional **ROBOTIC LIMBS** that watch what your natural limbs are doing and try to figure out what you need them to do. They could help you open a door when you have a heavy box in your natural arms or hoist that suitcase overhead on an airplane. Or maybe even catch that baseball flying at you in center field!

Think Twice!

How would you use multiple arms? Do you think you'd find them useful or ultimately a bother?

If you CHOSE ⬇ THAT:

Researchers at Weill Cornell Medical College in New York City are working on developing **ARTIFICIAL RETINAS** to treat blindness in people. The retina is the part of the eye that transfers information to the brain, enabling us to see. Light hits the **PHOTORECEPTOR CELLS** on the retina and is then converted into electrical impulses that are carried to the brain. An artificial retina, utilizing a **CHIP,** has already worked in mice and might work in people someday soon.

CHOOSE THIS:

Swim with sharks.

CHOOSE THAT:

Use poop for power.

MUSE BEFORE YOU CHOOSE

Big teeth. Renewable energy.

If you CHOSE THIS:

You can swim like a **SHARK** using a **WET SUIT** made of faux sharkskin. Scientists have replicated the toothlike scales called **DENTICLES** found on sharkskin through 3-D printing and created an inspired material. They've attached it to a robotic arm to check out swim speed. Scientists found that the skin reduced **ENERGY** expenditures and increased swimming speed. Researchers believe that it could one day be used to produce speedy swimsuits.

Choice Nugget

Poop has many uses. In Thailand, elephant poop patties are turned into paper and sold to raise funds for preservation projects, and in Africa, fresh camel poop has been used to cure dysentery. In fact, German soldiers used the remedy during World War II.

If you CHOSE THAT:

This might not rank up with wind and solar as **ALTERNATIVE ENERGY** sources at the moment, but poop power might have potential.

Researchers at Stanford University in California, U.S.A., have developed a way to generate electricity using sewage bacteria. This idea isn't new, but the researchers' methods have proven to be more efficient because of their use of **EXOELECTROGENIC** microbes. That means that the bacteria produce electric energy as they eat organic material (like poop). This process can be used at sewage treatment plants or to **BREAK DOWN** organic pollutants that threaten marine life.

LET'S SEE WHAT **YOUR CHOICES** SAY **ABOUT YOU.**

DOC TALK ...

PSYCHOLOGIST
DR. MATT BELLACE
DISSECTS YOUR
DECISIONS ...

ANALYZE
THIS!

If you mostly picked **CHOOSE THIS,** you're a fun-loving person who uses technology for amusement and intellectual stimulation. In your everyday life, you prefer walking around without electronic equipment buzzing in your ear like a starving mosquito. However, when you're hanging out with friends, you love it when they show you the latest technological tricks. You look at these cool gadgets in a very practical lighL. They're fun, but you feel that they're not a necessity in your everyday life and you'd rather spend your money on something else.

ANALYZE
THAT!

If you mostly picked **CHOOSE THAT,** you're a practical thinker who knows how to use technology to improve your life. Your personality is all about independence and doing things your way. You see technology as a tool to increasing your ability to break free. The only risk of this empowered lifestyle is that when the technology breaks down—and it always does—it could leave you very annoyed at the world. Remember to value experiences and not to put too much weight in material things.

CHAPTER 9

TRICK or TREAT?

You'll just have to take a risk when making your decisions in this chapter! Sometimes you end up with something wonderful, like a whopping bag of candy, but you could also end up with something gross, scary, or stinky! Pick your poison in this chapter. *Mwahaha!*

CHOOSE THIS:

Ride a bike.

or

CHOOSE THAT:

Take the train.

MUSE BEFORE YOU CHOOSE

Peddle away. Leave the driving to us.

If you CHOSE THIS:

You're in for a **TREAT** someday! The **SKYCYCLE** was a project first proposed in London in 2011 that would let you ride your bike in the sky on a 137-mile (220-km) futuristic **ABOVEGROUND BIKE LANE.** Although the idea was eventually rejected by London politicians for being too expensive, aboveground bike lanes are more than just a pipe dream. Urban transport systems like Sky-Cycle could **REVOLUTIONIZE** stressful urban commutes by making commuting safer and more approachable for cyclists than roads loaded with heavy car traffic. They'd be **ECO-FRIENDLY** too!

If you CHOSE THAT:

You've been **TRICKED.** The Silver-pilen, or **"SILVER ARROW,"** was built for Sweden's metro system but was left unpainted and was likely used only as a backup. It was rumored to be a **GHOST TRAIN** that screamed through stations after midnight without stopping and dropped passengers off months after they boarded.

CHOOSE **THIS:**

Kick a ball.
or

CHOOSE **THAT:**

Swing a bat.

Ted Williams ▶

MUSE
BEFORE YOU
CHOOSE

Powerful kicks. Powerful swings.

If you CHOSE ⬇THIS:

You're in for a **TREAT**. If soccer is your sport, Soccket the soccer ball does double duty. Not only can you **KICK IT** around a field, but when you do you can also **GENERATE POWER.** Playing with Soccket for just 30 minutes can produce three hours of power for a small appliance. It works like a self-winding watch that is wound with movement. It's already in all 50 U.S. states and 62 countries!

If you CHOSE THAT:⬇

You've been **TRICKED.** The baseball **BATS** favored by baseball great **TED WILLIAMS** and used by many major league hitters could be threatened. The wood for these bats comes from ash trees in the Allegheny Mountain forests, located on the border of New York and Pennsylvania, U.S.A., and an Asian beetle called the **EMERALD ASH BORER** has already killed tens of millions of trees in southeastern Michigan alone. So be careful with that wooden bat—it may be **ENDANGERED!**

ash borer beetle

CHOOSE
THIS:
Eat out of a toilet.

or

At Modern Toilet, the pork hot pot is served in a miniaturized toilet.

CHOOSE
THAT:
Eat fresh-picked fruit.

MUSE BEFORE YOU CHOOSE Smelly. Ripe.

If you CHOSE ↓THIS:

You're in for a **TREAT!** You won't have to eat your ice cream in the bathroom, but it will come served in a toilet. The **MODERN TOILET** restaurant in Taipei, Taiwan, serves up its foods in toilet-shaped **BOWLS.** Don't be afraid to try the "Green Dysentery," topped with a **SWEET KIWI** sauce.

If you CHOSE ↓THAT:

You've been **TRICKED.** Durian, the "king of fruits," is sold from stands in Southeast Asia, but it's banned from most hotels and public buses because of its **STINK.** It's known as the stinkiest fruit in the world. A single **DURIAN** smuggled into a hotel room may necessitate a **THREE-HOUR** cleaning with an air ionizer to eliminate the odor. That doesn't stop people from treating the fruit as a treasured delicacy.

durian fruit

CHOOSE **THIS:**

Eat a **soft**-boiled **egg.**

or

CHOOSE **THAT:**

Eat **food** **you hate.**

MUSE
BEFORE YOU
CHOOSE

Rich and creamy. May be healthy.

If you CHOSE ⬇THIS:

You've been TRICKED! This soft-boiled egg is different from what you may be used to. *Balut* is a common STREET FOOD in the Philippines and Vietnam. It is made with fertilized duck eggs that have been allowed to grow for a few weeks. The resulting soft-boiled egg also features a tiny FETAL DUCK complete with small bones, feathers, beak, and head. Most people slurp them right up from the shell with just a pinch of salt.

If you CHOSE ⬇THAT:

You're in for a TREAT! Not crazy about your dinner choice? Time to get creative with what's on your fork! The AROMAFORK allows you to try 21 DIFFERENT AROMAS, like basil and coffee. As you eat the food on your fork, the handle adds aromas for your brain to analyze. The result is said to ENHANCE your food and trick your mind. Imagine turning that bland potato into a culinary masterpiece, without having to add any condiments!

Choice Nugget

Our taste buds can detect only sweet, sour, bitter, and salty (and the less well-known umami) flavors, but our noses can tell the difference between thousands of flavors! Hurrah for our noses!

Myrtles Plantation, St. Francisville, Louisiana, U.S.A.

If you CHOSE ⬇THIS:

You've been **TRICKED!** The historic **MYRTLES PLANTATION** in St. Francisville, Louisiana, is one of the most **HAUNTED** houses in America according to the National Park Service. It is believed to be the site of a murder and many other natural deaths. More than ten **GHOSTS** are thought to haunt the property, including the ghost of a former slave named Chloe. Time to call Ghostbusters!

If you CHOSE ⬇THAT:

You're in for a **TREAT.** No needles at this hospital. It's frightfully fun. The **GHOST HOUSE** in Japan is in an abandoned hospital. Unlike your usual haunted house where you follow a set path through the rooms, here you can wander around freely. Like a movie set, this house is designed to **SCARE.** There are traps, ghosts, and screams around every corner. It's full of little episodes that will make you believe you've stepped right into a **HORROR** movie.

CHOOSE THIS:

A gingerbread house

CHOOSE THAT:

A house made of straw

MUSE BEFORE YOU CHOOSE

Tasty treat. Huff and puff and blow the house down!

If you CHOSE THIS:

You've been **TRICKED.** This isn't the gingerbread house that sits on your holiday table. It's **ACTUAL-SIZE.** And with that size comes nearly 36 million calories. The house is so big you could actually live in it. It was built in **TEXAS, U.S.A.,** and measures a whopping 60 feet (18 m) by 42 feet (13 m) and is 10 feet (3 m) tall. It was made with 7,200 **EGGS,** 3,000 pounds (1,360 kg) of **SUGAR,** 1,800 pounds (816 kg) of **BUTTER,** and 7,200 pounds (3,266 kg) of **FLOUR.** Only Hansel and Gretel would take a bite out of this one!

the world's largest gingerbread house in Texas, U.S.A.

If you CHOSE THAT:

You're in for a **TREAT!** This isn't a straw house a wolf can blow down. Houses that use straw bales as insulation are more **ENERGY EFFICIENT** than standard houses because the packed straw provides better insulation. **STRAW BALE HOUSES** also use stalks that otherwise would be burned as waste. So it's resourceful and eco-friendly!

builders using straw for insulation

CHOOSE THIS:

Spend a weekend on a deserted island.

or

CHOOSE THAT:

Spend a weekend in a ghost town.

MUSE BEFORE YOU CHOOSE Sun and sand. Spooky neighbors.

golden
lancehead
snake

If you CHOSE ⬇THIS:

You've been **TRICKED.** Ilha de Queimada Grande off the coast of Brazil might sound like a wonderful place for a visit, but it didn't get its nickname, **SNAKE ISLAND,** for nothing. This beautiful, deserted island just happens to be home to the world's most venomous **VIPER,** the golden lancehead. This snake doesn't just make your skin crawl, its bite actually makes your flesh rot right off the bone. No wonder the Brazilian government **FORBIDS** anyone from visiting the island without a doctor. Perhaps watch a scary movie instead?

If you CHOSE THAT:⬇

You're in for a **TREAT.** You can actually vacation in a real-life ghost town in Gold Point, Nevada, U.S.A., and experience a little bit of the **OLD WEST.** Your stay in a historic **CABIN** goes toward preserving and restoring the town. And there's plenty to do, including touring the town and **FOSSIL** hunting!

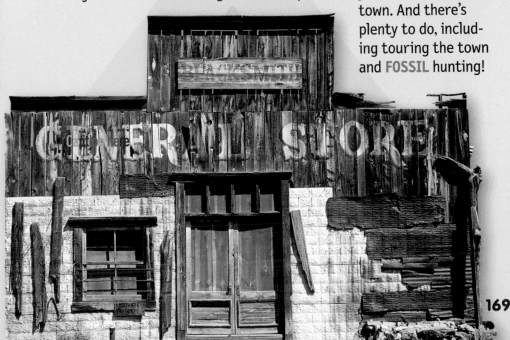

CHOOSE **THIS:**

Swim with giant **sharks.**

or

CHOOSE **THAT:**

Swim with **stingrays.**

MUSE
BEFORE YOU
CHOOSE

Jaws music plays in your head. Gentle giants?

whale shark

If you CHOSE
⬇THIS:

You're in for a **TREAT!** This may seem like the obvious trick, but swimming with **SHARKS** at Isla Mujeres in Mexico is definitely a treat! Most sharks are **NOT MAN-EATERS,** and the sharks that swim around this island are plankton-eating **WHALE SHARKS.** You can swim so close to them that you can see the beautifully patterned pale yellow dots and stripes on their skin. The best way to swim with these gentle giants is with snorkel gear.

If you CHOSE THAT:⬇

You've been **TRICKED.** Although swimming with these majestic **STING-RAYS** is a popular excursion, they can be very dangerous, even **DEADLY.** A famous Australian naturalist was killed by a stingray barb. You should **NEVER** swim directly over a stingray. Its **SHARP TAIL** with serrated barbs is used for defense when it feels threatened. The largest manta rays, on the other hand, are much larger but do not have stingers like stingrays.

stingray

Think Twice!

Ocean creatures should always be respected. Check out reputable establishments for any wild adventure.

I ♥ ANIMALS

171

ANALYZE THIS!

If you mostly picked **CHOOSE THIS,** you're an active person who makes cool choices whether you get tricked or not.

In life, things don't always turn out the way we plan. All you can do is make good choices and hope for the best. As you've figured out, when you err on the side of choosing things that will keep you moving and having fun, chances are you'll be treated more than tricked.

ANALYZE THAT!

If you mostly picked **CHOOSE THAT,** you're someone who takes pride in being different from the rest. Whether you're tricked more than treated doesn't matter to you; fitting in was never your main priority. You may be popular in school because some of your unusual choices lead to some very cool stories, but that doesn't impress you. At the end of the day, you like to move toward things that others avoid and think, "I can't wait to do that!"

Credits

Matt Bellace illustrations by Joe Rocco.

Cover: (painter palette) Jut/Shutterstock; (camera) Hugolacasse/Shutterstock; (colorful burst) David Arts/Shutterstock; (panda) GlobalP/iStockphoto; (frog) Kuttelvaserova Stuchelova/ Shutterstock

Staff for This Book
Ariane Szu-Tu, *Project Editor*
Julide Dengel, *Art Director*
Simon Renwick, *Designer*
Hillary Leo, *Photo Editor*
JR Mortimer and Nancy Castaldo, *Writers*
Michelle Harris, *Researcher*
Paige Towler, *Editorial Assistant*
Allie Allen and Sanjida Rashid, *Design Production Assistants*
Colm McKeveny, *Rights Clearance Specialist*
Michael Cassady, *Rights Clearance Assistant*
Grace Hill, *Managing Editor*
Mike O'Connor, *Production Editor*
Lewis R. Bassford, *Production Manager*
George Bounelis, *Manager, Production Services*
Susan Borke, *Legal and Business Affairs*

Published by the National Geographic Society
Gary E. Knell, *President and CEO*
John M. Fahey, *Chairman of the Board*
Melina Gerosa Bellows, *Chief Education Officer*
Declan Moore, *Chief Media Officer*
Hector Sierra, *Senior Vice President and General Manager,
  Book Division*

Senior Management Team, Kids Publishing and Media
Nancy Laties Feresten, *Senior Vice President;* Jennifer
Emmett, *Vice President, Editorial Director, Kids Books;* Julie
Vosburgh Agnone, *Vice President, Editorial Operations;*
Rachel Buchholz, *Editor and Vice President, NG Kids maga-
zine;* Michelle Sullivan, *Vice President, Kids Digital;* Eva
Absher-Schantz, *Design Director;* Jay Sumner, *Photo Direc-
tor;* Hannah August, *Marketing Director;* R. Gary Colbert,
Production Director

Digital Anne McCormack, *Director;* Laura Goertzel, Sara
Zeglin, *Producers;* Jed Winer, *Special Projects Assistant;*
Emma Rigney, *Creative Producer;* Brian Ford, *Video Pro-
ducer;* Bianca Bowman, *Assistant Producer;* Natalie Jones,
Senior Product Manager